BEYOND
THE FENCE

Nazmin Zaffar

ISBN 979-8-89186-346-0

CONTENTS

INTRODUCTION

My name is Naz, and this is my story. To many, it might seem like a common one. However, I am writing it so that someday, when you feel there is nothing left, I can come as a ray of hope. A hope that you can find in times of despair and pain, knowing that someone else has survived the same and so can you.

The world, as we all know, often smiles with the happy. But what about those who are struggling? That's where my story comes in. It serves as a protector, shining upon you like a ray from heaven. It is sent by someone from above who loves you deeply.

Bold and unwavering, my story is here to remind you that even in the darkest moments, there is always a glimmer of hope. It is a testament to the strength of the human spirit and the power of resilience.

So, when you find yourself lost and downtrodden, remember my story. Let it be a beacon of light, guiding you towards a brighter tomorrow. You are not alone in your struggles, and you too can overcome them.

I have always been a natural giver, even from the moment I entered this world. As a child, I would joyfully give away everything I had just to see the happiness it brought to others. And as I grew into adulthood, I never held back anything that could bring even a glimmer of joy to those around me. It was this unwavering desire to serve others and change the lives of the less fortunate that eventually led me to establish my very own non-governmental organisation (NGO).

There is a well-known saying that the doors of heaven swing wide open for those who selflessly serve others. And let me tell you, it couldn't be more true. The sheer happiness and fulfilment that comes from being a giver far surpass anything one could ever gain from being a taker.

In the pages of my forthcoming book, I invite you to embark on a journey with me. A journey that will take you from the innocence of my childhood to the person I am today. It is a journey filled with gratitude for the life I now lead, a life that can only be truly appreciated by sharing the intricacies of my own experiences. Within these pages, you will find tales of both joy and sorrow, of mistakes made and lessons learned, of blessings bestowed, and, ultimately, of acceptance.

My hope is that this journey of mine will not only inspire you but also make you stronger. By the time you reach the final chapter, I want you to feel a renewed sense of positivity coursing through your veins. I want you to discover the presence of your loved ones in your life like guardian angels watching over you.

So, brace yourself for an extraordinary tale of resilience, compassion, and unwavering determination. Together, let us embark on a journey that will leave an indelible mark on your soul.

"Beyond The Fence" is a profound compilation derived from the journals I have meticulously penned since my early childhood. Within its pages lies a treasure trove of factual accounts and real-life incidents, meticulously transcribed from my thoughts of yesteryears. This literary masterpiece delves into the profound moral lessons that underlie life-altering moments. It explores the indomitable strength that emanates not from triumph but from the arduous struggles and excruciating pain one endures, yet chooses never to succumb to.

I am eternally grateful to every individual who has played a pivotal role in shaping the contents of my journals, for it is their unwavering support and influence that have paved the way for the creation of this remarkable book. Though physically absent from my life today, their presence remains steadfastly by my side. I extend my heartfelt gratitude to my beloved parents and dear Mina, whose unwavering love and guidance continue to inspire me. Equally deserving of my appreciation are those remarkable individuals who remain steadfastly by my side, refusing to abandon me even in the face of adversity.

MY CHILDHOOD MEMORIES

I come from a family of four siblings, two sisters and one brother. I was the youngest of all, and I can say I was often pampered, but also the most responsible. Even today, my survival reflects on my upbringing, and the fact remains that your life shapes up only after you realise what's needed most and decide to move on.

I take you back to the days when I was growing up in Kohima, the land as green and the people as generous as they are even today.

All throughout my growing days, I would see relatives and friends visiting us with bags full of food and everything else that was available, probably from their farms and gardens. I would always think to myself how generous humans are and what a good world God had made. The large-heartedness of people I still remember, and it brings back memories that have made me what I am today.

My dad always said, "whatever you have, share it with others; you will never fall short because God provides."

The memories I cherish from childhood are mostly from Kohima. Here is a glimpse of what I remember as gifts that would come home: live chickens in a handbag, a drum full of live fish, a basket full of plums, pears, peaches, bananas, every kind of greens and fruits from the garden, larva, Mudi, Samuto, bison, venison, and wild fruits and mushrooms. The extra lot of cakes and gifts during Christmas, also the hand-carved articles, a few of which I still have, like the walking stick with a man on top and a stone knife.

My parents passed away, and I kept what I cherished most that reminded me of them, the Konyak walking stick and the stone knife. I take a glimpse of them every now and then and put them away safely. As a child, I was very scared of the stick because it had a man carved on the handle. I always thought that the man was looking at me. The stone knife was a carved sharp stone, which was always kept in the safe at home. No one knew where it actually came from. Mom said it was passed on to her from her dad, and grandpa got it from his dad. Now it's with me.

Something else that I kept in a little box in my drawer was dad's reading glasses and his last ECG strips. Also, some of his letters dated back to 1993 and 1996. I will share the letters with you. I kept Mom's reading glasses and hair clips in that box. Sometimes when I break down, I hold the box and cry. I miss them so much. Death changes everything, time changes nothing. I still miss the sound of their voices, the wisdom in their advice, the stories of their life, and just being in their presence. So, time changes nothing. I still miss them just as much today as I did the day they left me.

Now, after so many years, it still continues. My friends and family still send me parcels of food every time they remember me. They haven't given up on me even though I live so far away and am too lazy to follow up. Their packages contain everything they can lay their hands on, knowing that anything means everything to me. A few years back, when we had a school get-together, they kept a table full of food prepared to look like school-time junk, only for me. Sometimes life doesn't give you what you want, not because you don't deserve it, but because you deserve so much more. There is something beautiful about having long-term friends who have witnessed multiple versions of you and loved you unconditionally through each version.

Today, I have my own NGO where I look after many street children and homeless families in Mumbai, as well as counsel suicide victims and help restructure lives. It all started from what I learned as a child. It will never leave me; the memories will always stay, and so will my work as a lightworker. I am still in touch with my school friends, my old neighbours, siblings of friends who are no longer with us, or people whose parents remember me from somewhere. This is how they reach out – generous, always giving, never giving up on me. Many people found me on social media and got in touch with me. They remember me so clearly, though I have forgotten many faces.

My prayers are for every soul who has made me what I am today. Growing up in Kohima and then the many places around the world that all had memories, but the few things I will never forget about my Kohima are the things I hold onto even today, and they have helped me find my goal. I will always remember the kindness and generosity of people, the cold mountains with the sound of the breeze blowing, the beautiful flowers, and the warmth of people who stand by you at all times. A big buzzing house full of happiness. To me, Kohima is the memory I would take with me to my grave, knowing that what gave me immense joy is where I would like to return. "Dance before the music's over, live before your life is over."

As the youngest among my siblings, I was the last one to enrol in school. Mom and dad were working, and everyone else was in school. I was home alone with the helpers, and that's the only memory I want to forget. Sometimes I feel it was the freedom the helpers got when both parents worked, and they were on their own with no one to monitor them. This is why I never wanted to work full-time, leaving kids alone at home. I remember how the entire environment would change at home the moment everyone left for school and work. I would dread that feeling but had no choice as I was too small and didn't know what was happening. One day, dad came home early and saw how the house was left in disarray, and no one really looked after me. He not only fired all the servants but never left me home alone. I was sent to school much before the age of school, just to play with the nuns and wait for school to end to come home with my sisters. I would go with a tiffin and a water bottle every day and play around, visiting classrooms with the nuns and getting all the attention.

Little Flower School was a girls' convent school located on top of a hill. The beautiful meadows and mountains, the far away roads that it looked upon, and the path that was filled with daisies and cherry trees. The winter chill where the cheeks go red and the hands freeze, but the mischief and pranks never end. The punishments and bunking school to sit near the valley only to chat. How I wish I could once again relive that memory.

School is where I first learned to stand strong. It is where I first cried for friends when we separated, it is where I first decided to be a pilot and I was so cheered and admired. Amongst all the mischief, there was so much hope that floated around; the hope that everyone would do well in life without any prejudice. Also hope of joy where no one had to see a day of sorrow. This stayed with us till we parted and still remains. Even today, someone or the other calls me to ask if I am doing fine. They forget their own sorrows but remember mine. It's extremely rare to find friends who care about you without any agenda. They wish to see you achieve your dreams, encourage you to grow, and stand by you no matter what. I will never forget the support given to me by my friends and will always be grateful to them and keep them close. Life is too short to surround yourself with people who don't match your energy. My friends make me feel like sunlight. There is no jealousy; we share each other's pain and happiness. They encourage me to grow and want to see me succeed. They bring out the best in me and are always rooting for me. Such friends are not easy to find.

There is something so beautiful about having people who see the shift in you and encourage you to move ahead. Being happy doesn't mean you have it all; it simply means you are thankful for what you have.

My principal, Sister Annie, always boosted me and was my biggest support during my childhood days. I made it a point to always visit her during my travels. She would remind me of my dreams and how I should conquer every obstacle in my path, knowing that I have a greater purpose. She was the first to teach me about loyalty, strength, gratitude, and the fulfilment of God's wish. She said we are all here for a purpose and we should find it and fulfill it. Sister Annie used to say my purpose was special and I had to work harder than others. She passed away after many years, and I carried her coffin on my flight from Calcutta to Guwahati. I couldn't hold back my tears in the cockpit; I cried so bitterly on that short route. She was from Chennai, but her last wish was to be buried where she served most of her life.

Many friends from that time are no more; it's like a full generation has been wiped off. Every time I talk to someone, I get the news of someone's death. My prayers are for all of them. Today, after so many years, many of them still call to remind me of old days. Khati from New York and Binita from London, call to pep me up with old memories because they know I miss them and I am alone. They themselves are far from home, but it doesn't stop them from cheering me up.

When mom passed away, many of them came to visit me, and that was the last I saw them. It's been years since I haven't seen them. I will visit them; let some time pass when I am a little off work, I will visit them at their homes. Their children are all grown up. They talk about me waiting to see me, and it's the same with my cousins. We wait to see each other, and every phone call ends with: "Waiting to see you, please make it this Christmas."

My cousins and my aunt (Mahi) are so dear to me. Mahi is still in perfect health and knows everything. Whenever we speak, she worries about me, so I pretend that all is well, but I know that she knows I am now alone with the kids. She always reminds me that even if mom is no more, she is there and will always look after me. Moments where I should be comforting her, but instead, she comforts me. My cousins were very close to me when we were growing up. We were of the same age and shared the same stories and likes. Our houses were next to each other, so at one time we used to spend days and nights together, hopping from one house to the other, sharing food, clothes, and many secrets, till I had to leave. My Mahi reminds me of mom. I hugged her and cried when I left her the last time. I will go back to see her soon.

I had a cousin, K, who is no more, but I remember every time he came home to visit me during my visits, he would carry live chickens and fish for me, saying he just caught them from his farm and fishery for me when he heard I was home. I would always carry a t-shirt for him, and he would remind me that the last t-shirt I got him was still well-kept. These gestures I can never forget, how big-hearted people can be, knowing that there is not much in return. My other cousin, who was a Gambura (chief), had kept a bison horn for me from his son's wedding. He thought I could carry it back with me. The best gift I ever received.

The last time I visited Kohima, I didn't have my own house anymore since we shifted to Guwahati after mom and dad passed away. But I stayed at every cousin's house. They would pick me up and also drop me off at the next cousin's house so that everyone had a chance to be with me for a meal, and in-between, I could meet just a few friends because of a lack of time.

Up until a few years back, I would visit Kohima during the Hornbill Festival. It was an excuse to visit friends and family, and whoever got to know I was coming would visit me from wherever they were. At least this way, there was a get-together with friends. The Hornbill Festival is celebrated from the first to the tenth of December every year. It's a cultural festival very well-known all over the world for its location, beauty, weather, cultural activities, food, and, most of all, a never-seen performance. I love visiting every stall at the fest and sipping Zutho, the local rice wine, to be had in bamboo mugs. The food is something you would never find anywhere else, such as different innovative local delicacies. But the last time I was there, I saw a few stalls of Korean food, and I thought to myself, the noodles can't be better than the axoni. If you haven't visited the Hornbill Fest, it's a must, at least once you should take out time and visit.

I recall visiting my village in Assam called "Puranigudam" every holiday where we celebrated Eid in a big family gathering till one after the other, an elder passed away, and the gatherings became smaller until there were no more. There were no more Eid gatherings as no one wanted to visit Puranigudam from the big city.

One of my favourite memories from those days was sitting outside the main door with a bag of rice and a small cup. I would pour a cup of rice into each person's bag who came to ask for alms. Sometimes I would give them two or three cups if they needed it. This simple act of giving brought me so much happiness. While my cousins were busy playing, I found joy in helping the poor. I was always satisfied with what I was doing. Sometimes, when the rice ran out, I would ask my Big Aunt for another bag. She would refuse, saying it was for us and not for them. But I would insist, saying, "I won't eat, so give my share to the poor people." The poor who came asking for food were never satisfied and always asked for more. So, I would try to find ways to sneak them cakes and pithas, just to see them momentarily happy.

Puronigudam was close to Kaziranga, the wildlife sanctuary. All I could remember was how green and full of pukhuri (pond) it was. Spotting a Rhino was not unusual; we could see them from close by, grazing for hours. The herds of elephants too were peaceful and non-interfering. When we saw them, dad would say they brought us luck. Summers were extremely hot, and we had to live in a village style when we visited. The oil lamp, open baths, feet full of mud, etc., were part of our daily routine until there was proper electricity and sanitation. I remember our house had many trees of mangoes, jackfruit, leche, guava, custard apples, and star fruits, coconut, betel nut, and they were all sold to traders in advance. Every day a man would come and count the fruits and take them when they were ripe. We were told not to have them from the trees, but that is what we always did! We feasted on them when we visited.

Tomorrow, on Eid, I will be giving 1000 kg of rice and dal to the poor families living in the streets of Mumbai and burgers to all the children. I have an NGO that gives me exactly the same feeling as my good old Puronigudam, and though dad is no more, I still cherish his memories and follow his footsteps and sayings: "The poor are no less human; give them a little more than what you can afford; they need it more." I vividly remember someone from the nearby mosque would approach my dad for help, and the next thing you know, he'd be buying them a bicycle. When my mom questioned the necessity, since the person lived in the mosque, my dad would reply that they could use it to visit him. After all, he walked to the mosque every day.

It's that very mosque where my parents are buried in the kabarstan (burial place). Although women aren't allowed in, I always make it a point to visit their graves whenever I'm there. They don't say anything, but instead, their cycles serve as a reminder of the kindness my dad showed them.

These countless childhood experiences have shaped me into the person I am today. I'm grateful for the wonderful memories I have and hope they never fade away. They allow me to cherish and learn from them while also sharing their impact with others. Because the most beautiful things in life aren't material possessions; they're the people, places, memories, and snapshots that fill our hearts with feelings, moments, smiles, and laughter.

Memories of Mom and Dad remind me of many things that have become part of my day-to-day life. I now teach my girls the same things. The only change is that many years have passed, and a few things sound very ancient, and I am reminded many times that almost forty years have passed. But those times will never come back. I only wish I had lived those times a bit more so that I get a bit of everything that's no more. I miss my parents; I always dream of them and get visions of them present alongside me. What must they be thinking, and how do I see them all the time? Such questions arise all the time, and the only answer is a prayer for their peace.

Wherever they might be, they should be at peace for the lessons they left behind that have helped so many.

I've been through tough times, faced hardships, and even lost myself along the way. But here I am, still standing, moving forward, and growing stronger every day. I'll never forget the lessons life has taught me. They've only made me stronger and reminded me of Mom and Dad.

Now, it's time to close the chapter on childhood memories, hoping they'll stay with us forever and that we can learn from them. It's all about finding joy and happiness, showing care and generosity, and ultimately gaining the physical and mental strength that propels us forward. It becomes the wind in our sails.

BABLI BAHAR

If you were to ask any person to think of a place in their lives where their childhood stood still and everything was idyllic and perfect, it would have to be Babli Bahar for me. It was the microcosm of our existence growing up.

Microcosm in the dictionary is a community, a place, or a situation regarded as encapsulating in miniature the characteristic qualities or features of something much larger. Babli Bahar was exactly that. Babli Bahar represented a community that came together from all walks of life to share in the joy of childhood, adulthood, games and sports, food, social gatherings, and celebrating milestones. But most of all for us as children, it was the place where we spent our most idyllic childhood, free from all the cares of the world.

So what exactly is Babli Bahar, and where did the name come from? Babli Bahar was an open space surrounded by high- and low-rise buildings, right in the middle of a busy neighbourhood called P.R Hill. It was inhabited by families from all across the country. My dad, who was a man far ahead of his time and with great foresight, decided to build a recreational space for children and families when he built these homes. 'Babli' was the name of a child who lived there, the sister of Bablu, and 'Bahar' means 'outside' or 'outdoors', so it literally means an outside space.

My earliest memory of Babli Bahar was of coming home from school, dropping my bags on the dining room table, washing my 'haath muk,' meaning hands and face, and having a quick snack sometimes accompanied by hot tea (yes, we drank tea as children growing up in India), and rushing outside to play in Babli Bahar. And the games were simple and innovative: Sometimes it was just playing Catch or Tag, other times it was Hide and Seek or Hopscotch, where we hurriedly made a big box of squares with chalk and used a prized flat stone as a 'shooter'. Also popular with the girls was 'Pathor' play, a game with five small rounded stones and multiple steps. It gave us achy hands but was a lot of fun!

None of these games needed any elaborate or expensive equipment. It was just playing on the ground with the simplest tools you could get your hands on. As we grew older, our games changed. Now there was more kopdi (kabaddi), badminton, cricket, football, and a few broken windows to tell the tale. Sometimes we didn't need to play at all. We just gazed around our surroundings that enclosed Babli Bahar. On one side was the sprawling town of Kohima, spread out with the tall red sphere that was the Ao church at its centre. On the other side was the helipad. It always excited us children when a helicopter made its landing in a cloud of dust. So far away and so majestic! The adults would nod knowingly and mutter 'The Governor is here or some other big shot is here...'

The view I liked the best and remember most vividly was the Aradhura Range of mountains that were visible on one side of Babli Bahar. As the day progressed into the evening, you could see the mist drop down and envelop the mountain top. It was a clear sign that it was time to head home, wash our 'haath muk' again, and sit down with our books for evening study.

The families that resided around Babli Bahar came from all around the country. Looking back, I am enthralled and inspired by my father's idea to let out his premises to The All India Radio Company, which was a Central government organisation that recruited employees from all over India. Hence, from a young age, we were exposed to people who spoke different languages, ate different foods, celebrated different festivals, and led different lifestyles. Yet they all considered Babli Bahar their recreational space, and adults and children alike converged there to relax, share a laugh, have a swig of hot tea, and a piece of gossip. It brought everyone together.

The advantage of being exposed to many different cultures at a young age is immense. As an adult, I pride myself on speaking four languages fluently and four languages to get by. Being exposed to different cultures at an early age in Babli Bahar has allowed me to assimilate and integrate myself into different cultures, feel at home, and build friendships and relationships with people from different nationalities and from all walks of life. I hope to instil in my children this richness of varied cultural experiences.

How can we forget our childhood memories of food? The strongest of our sensory memories is taste. I remember cold winter afternoons snuggling in our pyjamas and oversized sweaters, sipping hot tea and delicious spiced namkeens (snacks) with our neighbours. Our seats kept moving constantly to catch the last rays of the feeble winter sun. In the end, we were left with a full belly and very burnt faces. Sometimes we were invited to partake in a family's lunch, and that was quite the happiest moment in our day. At other times, we chose a quiet moment to sneak some mango pickles that were drying in the sun. Oh, how good they tasted!

These were some of the foods we tasted from the Babli Bahar families:

- Tehri from the Shrivastav family from UP
- Rajma Chawal from the Khurana family from Punjab
- Chitol Maach from the Das Gupta family from Silchar
- Mooli Paratha from the Verma family from Punjab
- Irumba from the Hemro Singh family from Hojai
- Mutton Soup from the Das family from Kalimpong
- Baigoon Bhaja from the Debnath family from Kolkata

As time elapsed, Babli Bahar found more elaborate ways of bringing families together. Families spent birthdays and cultural festivals there. The walls around the playground were spruced up with lights and fresh paint during such occasions. When television had yet to make an appearance (Yes, there WAS such a time), I remember my dad occasionally borrowing a huge projector from the Publicity Department and showcasing Hindi movies in Babli Bahar. Oh my! What an occasion that was. The whole neighbourhood ate their earliest dinner ever to make sure they got the best seats in the house. Some of the movies I remember watching were Ek Nazar, Anand, Hum Hindustani, and Mujhe Jeene Do. We laughed, we cried, we sang along to the songs. It made a lasting imprint.

It has been a while since I visited Babli Bahar, and I wonder if it still exists. I hope it does. I hope, in some small way, it is still bringing joy to the lives of little children playing happily in its grounds. For those of us who played on it, it is forever etched in our collective memories as the special place of our growing years.

VOICES OF DAD AND MOM

As I reflect on my childhood, tears well up in my eyes. Those were the days when I was blissfully happy, surrounded by a carefree and protected environment. I had nothing to worry about, and the stress of that time now seems bittersweet, innocent, and true. It makes me wonder if the pain I feel today will also become innocent and sweet in a few years. It's strange how the heart works, but I don't want to get lost in this world and realise too late that I've lost touch with my innocent heart.

Losing my parents to cancer was the most devastating experience of my life. I was left with no answers, only an unending pain that seemed impossible to heal. I desperately searched for reasons and explanations, I tried reasoning and finding answers but in vain, I wondered how deeper any other pain would be compared to that of losing what meant the most to you.

I was all broken, still reasoning and wondering where I could have done a little more to stop what had happened, and just a few months after that, the news of Mina detected with cancer came in, I broke down into fragments this time. My elder sister who took mom and dad's place in my life was next. Mina, being the oldest, was very caring and strong. She was the pillar giving me support after my parents passed away. I never thought I would lose her too. She was only forty-nine and gone too soon. I was surrounded by loneliness and an empty world where I would only reason with myself as to why so much heartache. I would spend days without talking to anyone, I would wonder how to smile.

Death brings us close to our creator; we don't die when our heart stops but moments before it, and we are still there even after our heart stops. It's all because we stop to wonder if we have fulfilled our purpose. Everyone comes into the world with a purpose to complete a cycle of deeds after which they go back to the creator. The deeds are only to serve humanity; as a child, you were served because you were needy, and as an adult, you serve others because you can provide.

As you get older, you realise that you are not always right and there are so many things you could have handled better, so many situations where you could have been kinder and more aware of what needed to be done. All you can really do is forgive yourself and let your mistakes make you a better person. Thank the people who listened to me without judgement and loved me unconditionally. They could be no one else than your own parents. The biggest accomplishment for me in life would be to always follow how I was raised, never let the world change me, and also raise my children the same way. This is the only way to show gratitude to those who left us with the best values in life. In the modern world where every day a new generation comes up, the only way to preserve the values that built us is by listening to the inner voices of those whom we loved most in our life. And even if they are no longer with us, we should remember that only they cared about us unconditionally. They always wanted to see us achieve our dreams and encouraged us to grow, supporting us through all our shortcomings. My mind still talks to them. My heart still looks for them, but my soul knows they are at peace. I miss them every single day.

Dad always said, "Whatever you have shared with others, you will never fall short as God is there to provide."

My pain became my challenge, and I decided not to break down because I believed I was here for a purpose, and once the purpose was complete, I would be taken away. Till then, I will fight and stand strong no matter how difficult the road gets. I promised never to give up. Never forget the person you were. After the battles fought and the darkest moments passed, always be the person you were raised as. If the love you gave others is not reciprocated, don't worry; it will in some other way. Love always comes back in full circle. It will come back in some shape or form, and you will be there to see it happen.

During my saddest moments, I would pray to God, hoping for a glimpse of my mom and dad. Just one glance would have been enough to bring me comfort. Unfortunately, it never happened, and I had to learn to live with the longing to see them again and hear their voices. I convinced myself that I needed to move on because they always knew better and were guiding me from above.

As time went on, I started experiencing strange things. I would hear voices and see visions of things that were yet to come. At first, it didn't make much sense, but through meditation, I was able to open up channels and make sense of it all. It became clear to me that these voices were from someone who loved me dearly and was still watching over me. They were guiding me and reminding me that I was never alone.

On days when I felt inadequate, unloved, and unworthy, I would remind myself of whose daughter I was. Just the thought of my parents gave me the strength to keep going.

By this time, I had lost Mina also and was completely alone and shattered. She was my only support, and I had no one else left. She nurtured me after mom and dad died. She took care of me; she made sure nothing went wrong, and no one caused me grief because she knew it all. She knew I was suffering in my marriage, and it was going to end anytime, but she didn't want that to destroy me. I felt so safe in her presence; she stood so tall and protected me. She showed me my rights and made me aware that the wrong would never succeed. Till she lived, she made sure no harm came to me, but she was suffering, and it was terrible to see her trying so hard to mend my life when her life was slipping away.

I was still in the process of healing and recovering when I broke down once again. This time, all my hopes for diseases and modern medicines were shattered too. Whether it was chemotherapy, the latest drugs that showed promise, or even traditional herbal remedies, they were all just prolonging the inevitable and causing immense pain, which no one ever talked about. In my home, we never discussed the pain we were enduring, just to spare others from knowing. Can you imagine what people go through during cancer treatment? They hide their suffering, not wanting to burden others with their pain.

I performed the last rites for my mom and Mina, cleaning and bathing them before their burial. I witnessed what was left of them after enduring all those treatments. Cancer takes away everything from a person, leaving them with no choice. It doesn't discriminate based on age or whether someone is a mother leaving behind her children. It simply sweeps you away. We become so reliant on any new treatment that offers a glimmer of hope to save our loved ones from cancer. But in the end, we're left searching for answers to the never-ending questions of WHY and HOW.

There is a saying, "God forgives all those who suffer from cancer and opens the doors of heaven for them because He knows how much they have gone through."

I remember visiting Mom in Medanta Hospital in Gurgaon every time during her chemotherapy. I would leave the kids behind and take an early morning flight to Delhi, stay the whole day in the hospital, and return in a late-night flight to let the kids know I was home. Here I was, shuffling between kids and Mom, and in-between running all the other errands. I was never at rest, knowing that Mom was in the hospital, but for someone with kids, you are torn between responsibilities and emotions. My kids were small; they needed me, and Mom was so attached to me that I had to be there during her chemotherapy sessions. She would remind me many times, though I would already know. Being with her in her last few days brought back the time I couldn't spend with her. She would long to be with me, chat with me, comment on me, make fun of me, talk about old times, eat snacks with me, and, of course, our outings.

I would joke and laugh in the hospital room to keep Mom happy, but every chance I would get, I would sit on the stairs and weep. One time, Mom's doctor saw me weeping and came to talk to me, making me understand that those were her last few days, and I shouldn't let her see me cry. Mom saw him talking to me (apparently, she was walking around looking for me, which was told to me by the nurse later), and she took great pleasure in teasing me, saying that the doctor was flirting with me, that he keeps looking for me everywhere and finds a chance to talk to me. I kept nodding my head and rolling my eyes, which I used to do as a child to show my anger, but this time it was in pain.

Every time Mom was taken for chemotherapy, she would tell me that it's a small injection that would make her feel cold, that's all.

This is how she would hide her physical pain, but I knew what she was going through. When we got her back from the hospital because her last wish was to go home, she told me that she wanted a nice bath after staying so long in the hospital. I prepared her bath and helped her, not knowing she would catch a cold that would never leave her. She was on oxygen after that, and my biggest regret was that I should not have given her a bath. I made a mistake, I apologised, and I cried a lot. She removed her oxygen and told me that I should go home, visit the kids, and come back. She wasn't looking at me while talking, and I hugged her from behind and wept, saying I will be back with her favourite apples, and left. The next day she died. Her pain ended as God gave her relief, which is what I asked for, but I didn't know asking for relief from her pain would take her away from me forever and leave me with endless emotional pain.

She never left me; she stayed with me forever, loving me and being my strength. She said before leaving that every situation in life is temporary; the pain doesn't last forever. When life is good, make sure you enjoy it to the fullest, and when life is not so good, remember that it will not last, and better days are on the way.

I became very fragile after she left; people took advantage of the situation and tried to break me further, but the strong vibes from Mom guarded me, made me aware of what was going on, and kept guiding my path for the rest of my life. I could feel it in my soul when it was time. Time to move on from people, time to make a change in your life, time to get rid of unhealthy habits, and time to want more for yourself. It was a guided path.

I further realised that your loved ones who watch you only want you to stand strong, knowing that they are standing by you and will protect you. They want you to move on with life and find a way to resettle without them physically present but always there whenever you call upon them.

"We fall, we break, we fall. But then we rise, we heal, we overcome."

Losing someone you love causes pain that others wouldn't understand. Your emotions don't understand what's good for you; they only seek the presence of the lost and try every way to acquire them back. Those who deal with the loss remember who stood by them during their hard time and who didn't. They go to every extent to get justice for the wrong done to them in their time of grief.

No one has everything figured out. No one's life is easy and without struggle. It's human, and it's normal. It's okay to struggle. It's okay to be unsure and overwhelmed. It's okay to not have it together every minute of every day. It's okay to be exactly where you are and feel all the things you feel. You don't have to have all the answers or do things perfectly.

You just have to know that you are there. You hear the voices of those you love. You are living your life the way they taught you and left.

I never gave up on what I learned as a child. My prayers, my runs, my food habits, my homecoming before dark, my clean home, my respect for elders, my priorities, my children's happiness, my punctuality, my bedtime, my philanthropy, my strength, my studies, my habits, my fasting, my fit life.

THE ENDLESS SKY

To me, the motivation behind my flying is my dad. He always wanted me to do new things, bigger things. So, when I was thirteen years old, I learned to drive and got a licence. All of this was because dad was the Transport Commissioner, and he taught me to drive on a big helipad where he knew nothing would go wrong. He would say, "Start and do what you want," and I did as he said. Whatever I could do, I did. I stalled, skidded, forgot the clutch and gears, and the brakes until I learned. He would say, "Next, you will fly a plane," and soon after my 12th grade, he took me to a small flying club in Guwahati to fly. No time was wasted. Along with me, he did some flying hours too, first a joy ride, then some more sorties. He was most excited.

The Guwahati Flying Club had only one airplane, a Cessna. I never understood why one had to wait all day to fly for one hour and someday not even that. Your chance to fly in the queue of ten guys depended on how much patience you had and how respectful you were. I didn't have much chance, so I moved to Delhi, finished all my ground classes: Air Regulation, Air Navigation, Metrology, Radio Aids, and decided to go to a flying school in the US.

I went to Ft. Worth, Oklahoma, Orlando, and Dallas. My long flying journey in the US continued until I got my CPL Multi-Engine rating.

The first time I told Dad that I wanted to go to America to fly, I was only seventeen. He was anxious but a bit nervous, I could feel it. He kept saying that I was young, didn't know how to cook, the fees were expensive, and I wouldn't know how to stay alone, etc., etc. But he soon started to find positive answers for all his questions. For the first question about being young, he said that even he was young when he first started, so I am smarter and stronger than him. For the second question about cooking, he said I could learn to cook quickly before going, and anyway, everything is pre-cooked in the US, so it won't be a problem. For the third question about the fees, he said he would start some new business to get extra money and ended up buying a few buses. As for the last question about how I would stay alone, he came with me to America and stayed for a month, making sure he spoke to everyone, telling them to look after me, teaching me to take the school bus, pick up groceries, and finally settled me in an apartment and left.

So, this was Daddy, my source of strength, the one person who loved me unconditionally and the only person who overlooked my mistakes again and again, knowing that's how I would learn.

I've reviewed your text and made some minor grammar and punctuation adjustments while maintaining your writing style and using UK spelling conventions. Here's the edited version:

I flew all over the central and southern parts of America, building time and getting my ratings. I also studied Metrology, which kept me a little busy as I found it very tough to live alone. I missed home so much; everything felt so lonely. I kept listening to the few Hindi music tracks that I carried, which felt soothing but made me feel more homesick. Mom and Dad would call me every day through the telecom office. There was a guy named Alam who would connect them to me every day, and it became a routine call. Sometimes when they were not available, Alam would keep talking to me, making sure I was okay, and pass on any messages to them later in the day. During one of my visits home, I was told to get a gift for Alam, and I carried a souvenir for him.

There was nothing to do once school was over. You either go out partying with friends, work somewhere, or spend time with families if you have any. I didn't fit into any of these, so I kept to myself, playing basketball and going for runs until one day my school bag was stolen, and my passport went missing. Upon reporting to the authorities, I was given a work permit and a scholarship for a few subjects to make up for the loss because my return ticket had expired before my new passport came. I cried a lot because I couldn't come home and started working to earn money for a ticket. All this happened because in those days, foreign exchange was very difficult. Dad had to ask all his friends to find people who could give me money, and he, in return, paid someone here with interest. I had to count and use all my money carefully until dad could find someone to send me money. So, I couldn't afford a return ticket until I earned my own money. Every morning, I would work at a breakfast place and then go to school after earning a few tips. After school, I would study Metrology or work again. This was my life for a while, and I did all kinds of odd jobs in gas stations, delivery, restaurants, and ice-cream joints.

I later took a break from everything and started training for marathons. I would run at odd hours in different locations to build endurance, which I missed while running in Kohima. The weather was hot, and I was dehydrated all the time, but I made a few friends, and we would run together in places where there was water kept for runners. It was such a nice feeling, and for the first time, I felt that people were kind.

I met my running friends sometimes in the evenings. We would sometimes do an evening run on the path parallel to the runway and watch planes landing and takeoff. It was the most beautiful sight in my life. Also, at that time, the craze was Top Gun, so we started running that route more often just for the Top Gun-like feel, running next to a fighter taking off.

Then again, back to flying, and I do remember telling myself that someday I will "fly or run."

The first solo flight is very important and memorable to all. For me, it was memorable not only for me but also for my instructor. It was my first flight flying alone and his last flight, after which he joined a commercial airline. My respect to Capt. Bruno, who is now an examiner in Italy and has flown for many airlines Bruno was the tall, blue-eyed Italian hunk who was the most sought-after man in school. I would see all the ground trainers and secretaries flirting with him, and he would tell them, 'Not now, babes, I am busy with my student'. He was in India many times training pilots for an airline on a lease, but I never got to see him. We are still in touch. He calls me whenever he is here and is a regular donor to my NGO.

Facebook is where he found me after twenty-five years. He wrote to me to confirm it was me and showed me his logbook, where it was written "Nazmin Zaffar" flight timings. He said he had been looking for me for a long time and finally found me.

After my solo flight, I was on my own until I got my private pilot licence, so every morning in a calm sky, I would take a plane, build up some time alone in the controls, and return back happily. One morning I was told by the dispatcher that there was a cloud moving in but wouldn't be in my way. I didn't worry much and took off and was on my normal checks till I could see nothing outside, and since I was not instrument-rated, I couldn't fly in the weather, only looking at the instruments. The clouds had moved in faster than expected, and I was above the clouds, unable to see anything. This was a VFR (visual flying) flight, and I couldn't fly looking at the instruments. I was lost big time, saying my prayers. I tried everything to find my location, but all in vain. I even worked out where I would be at a certain time if I was visual, but that was getting more confusing as I was flying towards a clear sky, which was taking me further away. Though I knew that there was an international airport close by that I was not supposed to enter because of big planes landing and taking off, I never thought I would be entering that space. Finally, I see some ground, and I descend to go below the clouds, and the stall warning sounds because of my nose-down dive to find land. I pull up, and the stall warning comes again due to the rapid pull. Further, when I broke out of the clouds, the first thing I saw was the high-tension wires below me, so I concluded that I would die due to a stall or touching the high-tension wires, and in both cases, I would not survive. So, I say my prayers, and then I hear someone on the radio calling me. I quickly answer, and a squawk code is given. I squawk, and the Dallas International Airport guides me back home. The ATC controller asked me if I was lost and how many flying hours I had. I answered yes, I was lost and had sixteen hours. He laughed and said, Have a great day.

My Instrument Rating check flight was a total disaster. I ended up flying to the wrong airport where the examiner was supposed to meet me. And to make matters worse, it was pouring rain. I never imagined I would have to fly in such terrible weather just to get my Instrument Rating. I even tried to use the excuse of being sick, but the examiner insisted that I still had to go through with the check.

We decided to wait for the rain to stop, and in the meantime, he started asking me questions for the oral exam. But here's the kicker

- I could barely understand a word he was saying! He had this heavy cowboy accent that made it a real struggle for me. Talk about double trouble. Despite the language barrier, I managed to answer all his questions.

Finally, the rain stopped, and we took off. But the storm started heading back towards us. I couldn't handle the IFR flight, and his accent combined. It was just too much for me. I didn't make it.

A week later, I went back to the examiner. The weather was clear this time, and he didn't have any more questions for me. I walked away with my Instrument Rating.

Many months of flying and only flying passed with a PPL, Instrument Rating, CPL, Multi-Engine Rating, Boeing 737 200, 400, 800. Some days were good, some bad, some reminded me of my runs, some changed me to become more responsible, and yet some memories stayed forever. I would always tell dad about the interesting part of my flying, but some didn't go well with him, and once he almost pulled me out of flying after hearing my story. Then I realised he still had a soft corner, and it shouldn't be touched.

The story I had told him was about one of my cross-country flights to an airport up north called Kickapoo. In the middle of the lake during my descent, I saw an airplane sitting still in the transparent water. For a moment, it looked like it was on land because the water was so clear you could read the call sign and registration number of the Piper Arrow. I came back, and the dispatcher told me that it had crashed in bad weather a few days back and couldn't be removed. It felt so close and scary because my plane was smaller. This story scared dad, and he kept thinking that that would probably be the fate of his daughter. He had many sleepless nights and finally made his way to ask me to try another career.

When I finally got my Commercial Pilot Licence, I was not even 21. My name was in the newspaper as I was the youngest and first female pilot from the Northeast. The chief ministers of Nagaland and Assam met me and recommended my name wherever it was needed. My respect to them. I stayed on for a while, looking for a job, but those days it was tough to find a job in an airline as there were very few of them, and no private airline had started by then.

My next destination was Italy, as I had an open invitation to stay and help out in leasing out an airplane that was flown to Italy from Texas by a few of my friends when we all finished our flying. This decision was made because I was getting a bit frustrated waiting for a job opening, but my parents were not happy about it. I decided I would come back with more flying time and work at the same time to earn some money.

Italy was one of the most beautiful places on earth. Everything about Italy brought a happy memory: Turin, Milan, Ivrea, Tuscany, Venice, Rome, and the Alps, which was my solitude destination. I loved the food and the daily walks by the river with an ice-cream. The one thing about living abroad away from home is the lonely feeling that creeps up every now and then. After so many years, it still never left me. I would get homesick and miss every little thing from home. I would carry little trinkets that had some significance. I loved listening to Hindi-speaking people and talking to them just for the sake of speaking Hindi.

More than anything, I loved the Italian Alps. They reminded me of Kohima, the cool, biting, crisp air of the Alps. I would stay alone in the holiday home owned by a friend, with nothing to distract my thoughts. That's where I would sit every day to write. I felt my feelings and heart could only be heard by my book and pen. One such day, while I climbed the mountain and sat to write, I saw the

Italian football team Inter Milan get off a bus and start practicing their high-altitude drills. Pity I was not on social media at that time to take pictures; I don't know if it even existed.

One thing that stayed in my mind was that my family wasn't happy with my decision to settle in Italy, though I convinced them that I would be back whenever there was a job opening for me. To them, the only thing that mattered was they wanted to see me home. Every time I came home, I made sure I carried a warm cardigan for dad and flowers for mom. It was to show them how much I loved them. They would say to me, "May every sunrise bring you hope, and may every sunset bring you peace."

I came a few times to visit home, and every time I was here, I applied to every airline to make dad happy. I would again promise him that whenever any airline replies, I will be back. One day I got a call from an airline called Alliance Air; it was a subsidiary of Indian Airlines, and they wanted me for a ground job till I started flying. This came as a surprise, as I wasn't prepared to leave everything and come back as soon as an airline called, but my dad was at his peak of excitement, and he kept telling me I had promised and I had to come back and take the job.

It was a tough one for me, as all this time I was trying to settle in Italy and continue flying with Lorenzo. We were together at school, and he was the reason I went back to Italy. His family wanted us to get married and also tried talking to my parents, but dad's answer was that I needed to work and settle down first before getting married. Many new complications cropped up as I was getting emotionally blackmailed by both sides, but finally, I left everything and came back.

Alliance Air was based in Delhi, and that's where I stayed. In the first few weeks, all the memories I had been carrying all this time of coming back and settling in India started fading off. Delhi was a horrible place to live. I had a house in Defence Colony, and I started working there, but the problems I faced in those few months were enough to move me out and never return to Delhi. The streets were so unsafe for females that every time I was out, it became a habit to use a scarf and return home early. It was the most unsafe place. Working in a new environment was very tough, especially if you were a female in a male-dominated workplace. There was so much politics everywhere; everyone worked less and bitched about others more; it was like they were getting paid only for that.

I didn't enjoy staying and working there, so I joined Sahara next, which was nothing better. Then I got a chance to join Jet Airways, and I left for Bombay.

Bombay was a sea of change, a cosmopolitan society with everyone busy in their own lives. To me, this was a place I loved. I had a house in Khar, not too far from the airport, the sea, and Jogger's Park. I was all set with a place to fly and run. My ground classes had started. The initial training on the 737 simulator and DGCA exams were done here, then we were sent to Malaysia for training; everything was only study and flying. It was getting very tiring. I missed my leisure days. There were very few female pilots in those days, and the private airlines had just boomed. I had a few regular routes, and one of them was the Calcutta-Guwahati sector. I would always fly the last leg as an additional crew and get off in Guwahati for the weekend. Dad would always be at the airport to pick me up, and after spending the weekend doing nothing but eating, he would drop me back on Monday. I always asked him why he liked the airport drive so much, and he would smile and say it was an excuse to find the big fresh fish from the nearby fisheries on his way back home.

Later, when he was unwell, he was asked to avoid all his favourite food, and one of them was the big fish that he would come to the airport for.

I flew for a long time, but when other requirements gained priority, I took a break and somehow prioritised those, which appeared just as vital or more so. The vast sky and flying were things I missed. I would pause for a bit and transport myself back to the times when I was flying over the skies and experiencing the joyful surge of freedom. During those years without flying, I yearned for the feeling of being free and having only the sound of the wind around me. But now that life has calmed down, and those other obligations have been met, I find myself itching to flap my wings once more and fly away.

But it's time for me to sit back now as my daughters are getting ready to fly. It's probably another way of my passion and dream come true, seeing my girls follow in my footsteps and pursue their own dreams of flying. As I watch them prepare to take off, I can't help but feel a sense of fulfillment and pride. It's a different kind of joy, knowing that my passion has been passed down to the next generation, and I can't wait to see where their wings will take them.

AS LIFE GOES BY

They say that before something great happens to you, everything falls apart. This particular phase of my life shattered me and transformed me into someone unrecognisable. The person I had grown up to be seemed to vanish completely during this time until I began the arduous task of piecing myself back together. Despite the challenges, my life continued on its intended path, filled with family, friends, and the exhilaration of soaring through the skies in what I believed to be my true world.

It was during this period that I crossed paths with the man I would eventually marry. He, too, was a pilot, and I couldn't help but feel grateful to the universe for aligning everything so perfectly within my own realm. Although he belonged to a different airline, our shared background led me to believe that adjusting to our life together would be relatively effortless. The notion of marriage—continuing on without having to make significant changes—was a dream we all yearned for. And I, too, held onto this dream, convinced that our shared work environment would foster greater understanding and require fewer adjustments. However, as we embarked on our courtship, doubts began to creep in. The initial days were far from idyllic, and I couldn't shake the feeling that something was amiss. Yet, I clung to the reassurance that everything would fall into place once we exchanged vows.

It is often said that minor issues in a relationship will magically resolve themselves once they are married. However, this notion is far from the truth. It is crucial to understand that disagreements and conflicts should never be underestimated, assuming that marriage will miraculously fix them. Trust me when I say that building a foundation on the belief that things will improve after marriage is a recipe for disaster.

In my personal life, I found myself constantly trying to adapt to my partner's world, believing it would lead to a harmonious union. However, my efforts only resulted in pain and disappointment as I attempted to navigate unfamiliar territory. It felt as though I was crossing a metaphorical fence, leaving behind my own world, only to return battered and bruised. It is essential to recognise that a successful relationship requires open communication, compromise, and a shared understanding of each other's needs and values. Merely hoping that problems will vanish after marriage is a misguided approach that often leads to heartbreak and turmoil.

The first thing I lost was my job, followed by my friends, and eventually my family. My entire world underwent a drastic transformation, devoid of peace and happiness. I found myself merely conforming to the expectations placed upon me, oblivious to the fact that it was pushing me further and further away from my true self. Every interaction became an argument, filled with tension and hostility. Positive words were a rarity, as the focus was always on striving to be better in order to please those around me.

Meanwhile, his world remained stagnant and resistant to change, and he took pride in it. He refused to embrace anything new, not even for the sake of our children. I constantly reminded myself that this was not who I truly was, but with the responsibility of two kids, I felt like a burden, unable to adapt beyond the confines of my own world. I placed the blame solely on myself. As time went on, this cycle of blame and shame became an integral part of my existence. I began to accept and live in a reality filled with abuse and demoralisation, convinced that this was the new world I had created through my constant efforts to adjust to the initial misunderstandings. Threats, challenges, abuse, vengeance, dominance, and humiliation became the norm, overshadowing any glimmer of hope or positivity.

Building a relationship founded on false hope takes years, yet it can be shattered in mere minutes. What remained unresolved only grew, leaving no room for repair. I found it impossible to love a man who constantly demanded that I become a better person while disregarding my own world. Despite my efforts, I could never comprehend why I was deemed inadequate for him or what made him so self-absorbed.

I couldn't love a man who never saw anything in me. However much I tried, I couldn't figure out why I was so bad for him and what made him so conscious that he wouldn't care much about anything but himself. No matter what I tried, whether it was accommodating his lifestyle or prioritising our children, nothing seemed to work. Eventually, I reached a point of surrender, realising that I could no longer find any answers. I made the decision to leave him, allowing him the freedom to pursue his desires, while I moved on to a new chapter in my life.

THE SINGLE MOTHER

The single mother is often seen as broken or incomplete, going through the lows of life and destined to stay that way forever. But let me tell you, it's actually the complete opposite. She possesses a strength that surpasses everyone who has ever hurt her, and she will rise above it all once she finds her footing. Being a single parent is perhaps one of the toughest challenges any human can face. In my opinion, a single parent completely changes their perspective on life for the sake of their children, striving to minimise the impact of change and maintain a sense of normalcy. So, a mother fights through the hardships of life to level the playing field. She's never truly herself, always living and pretending for her children, so they can find the courage and strength they need. But behind that brave facade, only she knows the hidden sorrows she carries.

Deciding to become a single mother is an incredibly tough choice for any woman, as she knows the challenges that come with it. But once that decision is made, half the battle is already won by standing up against what's wrong. The other half is survival, and even that takes a toll on her. However, she was always prepared for it, fully aware of the consequences. She knew what was coming. After every disappointment, she will rise again because she refuses to let it linger. She's ready for the worst, knowing that what's best for her kids is also what's best for her. Her life is no longer her own; it belongs solely to her children's future.

Many memories pass by where one is reminded of the past with what goes on in the present, but sometimes the past is so horrifying that nothing in the present is bad enough to compare. It is best forgotten. Growth is painful. Change is also painful. But nothing is as painful as staying stuck somewhere you don't belong.

When the past only brings tears and you try to gather some memories that make you remember some good moments to bring in some change, you think to yourself: did it really happen, or am I just thinking? You forget about it, and this is how you start again with new memories that you know will always stay.

Looking back at the past, it becomes clear that two people with different needs and backgrounds rarely find common ground. Their priorities diverge, and sometimes you have to release those individuals who you thought were there for you, only to realise they never truly wanted the same things. It's better to let go and move forward. As time passes, the path widens.

When a relationship crumbles due to materialistic desires and unfaithfulness, the truth becomes elusive. Everything feels surreal, and there are signs everywhere—a certain look in the eye, a chilling sensation. These cautionary signals become too strong to ignore. It feels as though all the values that shaped you would be meaningless if you didn't take action. These are the voices of our loved ones, whether they are still with us or have passed on. They communicate with us in various ways, showing us signs. We must be perceptive enough to catch those vibes and react. But the moment we stand up for what is right for ourselves, we become condemned. We lose everyone who was once a friend, family member, or someone we believed cared for us. Everyone turns against us simply because we dared to react and fight for what was best for us and our children.

Your children would be taught to turn against you from an early age, all to protect the lies that have been told. Once it becomes known that you have gone against the man who everyone sees as a completely different person, you'll find yourself standing alone against the world. Your children and friends will be fed the worst possible things about you. I was labelled as a bad-character woman, a cheater, a thief, a bad mother, a bad wife, and someone with a bad upbringing. But in the end, all these accusations actually pointed towards him because that's exactly what he was doing. He took all my savings, had affairs with multiple women, neglected our kids, and had the full support of his parents in all his actions. Whatever he hated in me was missing in him.

All this hurt me very deeply, but I kept telling myself that it was my decision and I had to go through whatever came my way because the truth would be out someday for everyone to see. In all these times of making the toughest decisions, I missed mom, dad, and Mina the most. If they were around, everything would have been different. I wouldn't have had to depend on friends to stand for me, but it was all God's will, as in my eighteen years of marriage, every time I wanted to tell them about wanting to end my marriage, I couldn't as their health deteriorated and they left me. I could never tell them what I wanted, though they knew all along what was going on but were helpless. In their last breath, I heard them say they were scared to leave me alone; I must be strong. All three of them said the same thing. Maybe there was something to it; maybe they really wanted to do something for me but couldn't. That's why, after they passed away, I gathered all the courage and, with their help, stood up to fight a long battle all alone, knowing that they would protect me. When we start to get better, we also often feel sad because we start to realise how much we have missed out on, how badly certain people failed us, and what the younger version of us actually deserved.

There were friends who stood by me and helped me with decision-making as it was difficult deciding many issues with two children involved. But after a certain time, I realised that there were just two people left who stood strong by me, and all the others had left my side and gone to the other side. This again was a big hit on me as it took away my confidence, and the world once again seemed ruthless and selfish. I left them on their own and moved on. I don't chase people and friends. I worked hard to be myself. The right people who belong in my life will stay. It's during the worst storms of your life that you will get to see the true colours of people who say they care about you.

My parents were blamed, saying that this is the upbringing and that it's being implemented now. The kids were told their mother was breaking down the family and the house, she didn't care, she doesn't love. They were made to go against me, and this remained in their minds for a long time. Few people advised me on his behalf. I was told that women have to tolerate and go on with what goes on, they cannot react or agitate. I was told that men can do whatever they wish, and have as many partners as they want, but the wife need not say anything. I was also told that he was adjusting between his lover and me, and I shouldn't mind. I saw what was happening but did not react, not knowing how to tell the kids about it until one day when I went to pick up the kids from school, they asked me to leave him. They told me he was having an affair and they didn't want to see him. That day I decided to end my so-called comfort zone married life. It wasn't a big relief. My mind already knew. My heart was denying it for the sake of the kids, I just needed a go-ahead from them. I gathered the courage to sit down with them and explain my decision to leave him. As I poured out my feelings, their understanding and support gave me the final push I needed to break free from the confines of my unhappy marriage.

Not everything is worth fixing, especially when you have been completely shattered. Get hold of yourself and move on. The only reason people take you for granted is because they assume you will always be there. Prove them wrong. The path to parenting alone can be tough, especially if the support is not enough. Being with no one is better than being with the wrong one. Sometimes those who fly solo have the strongest wings.

You cannot change the past and the hurt you had to endure, but you can use the strength you gained from overcoming those obstacles to work towards making the best life for yourself. At your very best, you will still not be good enough for the wrong person. But at your worst, you will be good enough for the right person.

Being self-reliant is necessary in many situations that you have to face. If you find support in someone, it's a blessing. There are people who have gone through the same situation. Never think that you have to do it alone if you have someone who understands and is a part of the same circle, but that someone needs to be trustworthy and there for you whenever you are in need. It's so important that you stay positive and focused. Never forget how far you have come. Everything you have gotten through. All the times you have pushed on even though you felt you couldn't. All the mornings you got out of bed, no matter how hard it was. All the times you wanted to give up but you got through another day. Never forget how much strength you have learned and developed.

Never be a prisoner of your past; it was just a lesson, not a life sentence. When God made a woman fertile to have children, he made sure she was stronger than the others. A single mother has the strength and willpower of a few people put together. Whatever the circumstances might be that made her single, but the outcome is that she bears the burden alone. I am a single mother because I chose to be one; it was my choice to leave the man who was of no value to us but only caused pain in our lives. I am thankful that I am not where I used to be in life. I have outgrown and survived. It might hurt when you move on, but then it will heal. And with each passing day, you will get stronger, and life will get better.

Both my children are grown up now. They have seen and witnessed what happened in our life that broke our family, witnessed and testified in court, and received counselling and finally the verdict. All was seen and understood by them. I felt very sorry for what the kids had to go through, but there was no other option. I tried hard to keep them away from courts and witnessing arguments and decisions taken, but there was no other way as everything was documented, and it was known to them that he didn't want us anymore. Since then, I have tried so hard to ensure as much as possible that they are never hurt. I might break down, but I would overlook everything with a prayer and move on. I needed nothing for myself, so why hold grudges? All I want is to see them settled and happy.

As the years passed, we forgot the past as it didn't matter to us anymore. We became a small, happy family very attached to each other. We decided to stay in our old house and rebuild it, which made a vast difference in our lives because everything in the house was falling apart as we were shifting to a new house. It seemed like our house was exactly like what we were going through in life. So, I took time out and did up the full house, putting up wallpapers and painting and repairing the bathrooms and fixing broken doors and tiles, changing and replacing a few things, and finally, the house looked totally different. We all had a cosy corner, including Apple, our little puppy, Snowy, and Poppy, our cats, and Rosy, our turtle. It was a lot of work, but eventually, all was done. God didn't add days to my life because I needed it. He added it because someone else needed me.

The man remarried a young hostess from his airline and treated it as a prized trophy, for she was just a few years older than my elder daughter. We never communicated, except when it was time for the education fees. He would take that as an excuse to meet the kids, but we both knew what he had signed in court. He said he would never see the kids again because he was leaving them without any financial support. God forbid anyone from going through what I have gone through; yes, there are many cases worse than mine, but I really went through rough waters just to make sure the children were fine.

The kids were raised in a certain way, and I tried to give them the same lifestyle that they had before I became single so that they don't feel the pinch as if they had gone through a lot. I promised myself to love my children and never put them through anything that might hurt them again. To love them in their worst moment, their angry moment, their selfish moment, because it's in their most challenging moment that they need to feel loved.

My elder daughter matured with age. She is like a friend to me, a friend who left me when I needed her because of what was told to her against me, but now that she understood, she never left my side. She became my closest friend. I tell her about my problems, and she even resolves them. She also advises me. I love listening to her.

My younger daughter is still growing up and is very attached to me. I have seen her shed tears for me as she still remembers seeing me going through some bad fights. She is so mature and clever; I wait for her to come home from school and listen to her stories. I make her small snacks, which is what she likes after coming home. Then, after all the stories finish, she sits with her iPad and the pets a soft blanket, and a big smile that takes away all my pain. As kids grow, they become tied up with their own busy lives. I miss holding hands and our outings. They have become so busy, but I am still the same. Sometimes they understand that there is a vacuum, and we end up doing the same things again just for me. This is how they try to show me they care.

At times when the kids hurt me, I go to my room and shed a few tears in silence. I confirm with God that it's a temporary pain and the next morning it is gone. I can't hold things against them for long, as I understand that children are still learning and growing. Instead, I choose to focus on fostering understanding and forgiveness, knowing that their actions are often a result of their own struggles and challenges. This mindset allows me to approach each day with a fresh perspective and continue to nurture a positive relationship with the children in my life. I become as before: washing, cooking, cleaning, screaming, school, shopping, worrying, loving. It's a world for them, I have nothing for me here, my time is to make sure their world is a happy one, and I do everything for it. I find fulfillment in putting their needs first and seeing them thrive in a safe and loving environment. While it can be challenging at times, the joy I experience from witnessing their growth and happiness makes it all worthwhile.

Sometimes I wonder how I am surviving in this city all alone, just with two kids. It scares me, but I don't want the children to know that I am scared. Somehow, I manage to cover up; it's become part of my life. Putting on a brave face for my children's sake. Despite the challenges, I find solace in knowing that I am their pillar of strength and that my unwavering love will guide us through any storm that comes our way. I worry that the kids don't go through the same things I did. I teach them how to love, how to bond, how to deal with emotions, how to have healthy relationships, and how to get out of relationships that aren't healthy. The day the children become independent, my world will change, and I will move on to serve the Almighty. It's a promise I made, and till that day, nothing will happen to me—no health or wealth issues. Maybe this is the reason I am surviving through everything, just to give the children a good life and leave. If I could give my daughter three things, it would be confidence to always know her self-worth, the strength to chase her dreams, and the ability to know how deeply loved she is. That is what I can offer my kids after the lessons I have learned. The silent battles I fought, the setbacks I had to overcome, the dark days when I had to wipe my own tears and pat myself on the back

My story is filled with broken pieces, terrible choices, and ugly truths. It's also filled with a major comeback, peace in my soul, and grace that saved my life. People think that I keep going and don't get hurt. But I hurt, and I keep going. The heart won't feel this heavy forever, and someday soon this pain won't feel so overbearing. But for now, I need to stay strong and look beyond.

I pray my daughter is stronger than me. I pray she doesn't accept things I have accepted.

I pray she knows when to fight for something or someone and when to walk away.

I pray she never feels abandoned, unloved, or unappreciated. I pray she knows her worth.

I pray she knows how special she is, even if I am the only one assuring her.

I pray that she knows that no matter what, she always has me, physically or spiritually.

THE OTHER SIDE OF THE FENCE

"It's my road and my road alone, others can walk with me but no one can walk it for me." - Rumi

When God gives you a new beginning, don't repeat the old mistakes. When I first decided to end my marriage, it was after eighteen years of tolerating injustice and pain. I was a man who never stood by myself or the family, but I kept changing for the sake of the children until a day when I stood by the vibes that kept telling me to stand up and fight back even if I was on my own. The presence of inner strength and unseen protection made me gather the courage to put an end to the betrayal and inhuman treatment only a weak person would accept.

I was not weak, and I singlehandedly fought my battles, knowing that I had no family, only my two children. The effort taken to undo what was told to them against me gave me the courage to fight back against the man who made our lives miserable, but God had his own ways. My children saw and witnessed him go against us, which made them change their minds about what was told to them against me and believe in what was seen by them.

The only regret I had was that I should have done it earlier, but I forgive myself for taking so long to find myself, standing up, and moving on. I stood up for myself and fought alone. Life always gives you a second chance if you deserve one. I asked for one because I wanted to give my kids a new start and let them live life all over again. Sometimes you must hurt in order to know, fall in order to grow, or lose in order to gain because most of life's lessons are learned in pain.

I had to rebuild my whole life again. There were many obstacles in my path, and I had to live this life alone, with no one by my side. I had to learn to do everything on my own. First, I had to change names and addresses everywhere. I became a miss again. There was this air of calmness around; everything felt new and like it had never been done before. There was a feeling of freedom—not answerable to anyone, the decision-maker, the one in charge of everything, and finally the single parent. Maybe the journey isn't about becoming anything. Maybe it's about accepting everything that really isn't you so you can be who you were meant to be in the first place.

The society we live in gets very curious when they see a mother raising her kids singlehandedly. No one is ever satisfied without talking a little about someone who is starting a new life after a long struggle. They try to find out every detail about it by gathering all the available stories. In the beginning, it becomes a hot topic, but after some new interesting topic takes over, she is left alone. Then come the males, who suddenly think they have become a few years younger than before and take up the big challenge of getting friendly with you. They feel it's a big achievement. Also, according to them, someone single has a lot of free chatting time, and they try not to miss the opportunity. On the other hand, the wives are fuming and look like they would burst into flames. These exchanges of looks and talks continue for some time, then die down because of no responses. And yes, there is a long line of matchmaking that takes over every conversation that happens with certain people. They feel it's a way to show they care. I used to think that the worst thing in life was to end up all alone. But no, the worst thing in life is to end up with people who make you feel alone.

It took me a long time to realise that not everything in life is meant to be beautiful. Not every person we feel something deep about is meant to make a home with us and be together forever. Sometimes people come into our lives to teach us how to love, and sometimes people come into our lives to teach us how to not love. How not to shrink ourselves ever again and how to repeatedly make the same mistakes. Sometimes people leave, but their lessons always stay, and that's what matters. It's what we learn and absorb later. My relationship with myself is the hardest because I can't escape from my own thoughts and feelings. This means I have to come to terms with every error I make and accept every imperfection. It's essential to learn to love and care for myself, even during times when I am upset or disappointed with my actions because I have only myself to fall back on.

The reaction of people when they see someone single managing on her own is not very pleasant. Firstly, everyone is very curious about a new man in her life. Secondly, the question of what was in the divorce settlement always arises. Thirdly, what's the ex-husband up to lately? And lastly, whose fault was it? And, of course, passing judgements on everything possible. They even drag the kids in, pretending to care. At that time, all that's needed is a little quiet time, just on my own, enjoying the undisturbed life after a long struggle. The high people get from my life fall flat; no sooner do they realise that there's nothing much here. People see your peace and get envious, wondering how you bounced back from situations that would have crushed them. What they don't know is that the peace wasn't handed over to me. It's the result of hard work, struggles, emotional cuts, growth, and many other tear-filled nights.

My newly acquired peace continues. My home will be a home with no loud anger, no explosive rage, no slamming doors or breaking glass, no name-calling, shaming, or blackmail. My home will be gentle; it will be warm. It will keep my loved ones safe. No fear, no hurt, and no worries. I may come from a broken and twisted place, but I will build something whole and safe. I will happily do everything I need to do, knowing that it's for good now.

Sometimes the universe will ask you to be patient, not because it's punishing you but because it's protecting you from certain energies and preparing you for the next step.

You should never regret going after what makes your heart happy, even if it ends in hurt. You should feel so proud of yourself for being brave enough to chase what makes you feel alive. There are some people out there who are too afraid to chase their dreams and who admire the strength in you. You should feel proud of yourself for knowing what you want and taking steps to obtain it.

Some days life is just hard, and some days are just rough, and some days you just break down and cry before you move forward. My side of the story doesn't matter anymore. Life happened; it hurt; I healed; but most importantly, I learned. Don't wait for things to get easier, simpler, or better. Life will always be complicated. Learn to be happy right now.

At the end of the day, it is only me. I have to make sure that I am okay. It's me who has to hold myself. It's me who has to decide to keep going. I have to keep holding on and keep trying. It's hard to be alone out there, and I know it. I can do whatever I want to do. I am strong and have made it so far. This side of the fence feels so much better: calmer, quieter, peaceful, and positive. I need to hold on to myself and be patient. Everything will come to me at the right time.

I need to calmly get hold of my emotions and act accordingly since I am on my own.

In this next season of my life, I make it a point to live a little bit more. To spend more time doing the things I enjoy. To make more memories with the people I love. To step outside of my comfort zone. To make necessary changes. To take calculated risks. To explore the infinite opportunities that this world has to offer. There is so much to life than my day-to-day routine. In this one precious life I have been blessed with, I hope I commit to living in a way that truly makes me feel alive. I will respect myself enough to walk away from anything that no longer serves me, no longer grows me, and no longer makes me happy.

I am writing this and recalling the times gone. I feel I was only trying to make up for the lost times, especially for the kids, that I lost my own identity. My new one is that of a single parent trying to make a happy world for her kids. In the end, no one remembers a beautiful face or body, but everyone remembers the most beautiful soul, and that's what I want to be remembered as.

THE DAWN

Adobe Stock | #167476390

The storm in my life settled, and I had a chance to start life again with my children with no one to physically abuse or threaten me constantly. The hope that came to my life was after a long wait of tears and struggles. I gave up on all my extravagant needs and started realising what was actually needed to live in a world alone with two daughters, and I started working towards those needs. I finally realised who my real friends were and started giving them back whatever I had left in my basket, be it love, gratitude, or support, with a prayer for their happiness.

I also found more time to grieve for people I lost—people who loved me unconditionally, but I never made enough time for them, even after they passed away. I was always tied up in my own tangles and couldn't make time for them. I couldn't tell people who loved me that I did the same. All this realisation came in, and I blamed myself for not doing enough when they were there, but I asked for forgiveness as my life was a mess and I didn't make time to understand them, but I did now, though it was a bit late.

I went back in time, I went through the grief of losing everyone I loved, I thought of all our precious moments, and I even visited places that reminded me of them. There was certain food that they loved, and I avoided having it, but I started having it to feel closer to them. It was so painful; I relived the pain again because I felt I never mourned enough for them.

Losing someone you love is one of the most difficult experiences a person can go through. It is a time of grief and sadness, and it is not uncommon to feel lonely. This is because they are often our primary source of love, support, and connection. When they are gone, we can feel like we have lost a part of ourselves.

The feeling of loneliness after losing someone can be overwhelming. It can make us feel isolated and alone, even when we are surrounded by people who care about us. We may find ourselves withdrawing from social activities and relationships, and we may feel like we can't connect with others anymore.

There are a few reasons why loneliness is so common after losing a loved one. First, the death of a parent can be a very traumatic event. It can trigger feelings of sadness, anger, guilt, and fear. These emotions can be difficult to cope with and can make it hard to reach out to others for support. Second, losing someone can disrupt our sense of identity. Our parents are often our role models and our primary source of guidance. When they are gone, we may feel lost and unsure of who we are. This can make it difficult to connect with others on a meaningful level. Third, losing someone can make us feel like we are missing out on life. We may see our friends and family moving on with their lives, and we may feel like we are stuck in the past. This can lead to feelings of isolation and loneliness.

I was feeling lonely after grieving for the loss of all those I loved so much. It was important to allow myself to feel my emotions. I tried not to bottle up my grief or sadness, remembering that I was not alone. There is no right or wrong way to grieve, and it is important to take your time. With time and support, you will heal and find your way forward. The silent battles I fought, the setbacks I had to overcome, the dark days when I had to wipe my own tears.

I tried not to isolate myself. It is important to stay connected, even if it is difficult. I found new ways to connect with my loved ones. I started talking to them, writing to them, and visiting their gravesite. Focused on the positive memories I had of them. This helped me to feel closer to them even though they were gone. I gave myself time to heal. There was no set timeline. All I knew was that I slowly felt better, knowing that I did all that I could do this time. The most beautiful things in life are not things. They are people and places and memories and pictures. They are feelings and moments and smiles and laughter.

"The secret to change is to focus all your energy not on fighting the old but building the new." My new was a struggle but eventually, it all fell into place. I soon became stronger than I ever was and received lots of appreciation. Now the focus was on healing others. I started a group called "Uplift" for single parents, focusing on helping each other grow and supporting the one-parent community. Here there were only people who were single, unmarried, widowed, divorced, and those who supported. Finally, there were so many people who were the same as me, going through similar situations. I realised they understood me better, and the world was different. I fitted better here and decided to make the group bigger so that more people could join, and we all worked towards supporting each other.

When you fall, all you need to do is get up and start again. No matter the bruises and cuts, time heals them all. No matter the opinion of those who saw you fall, all that matters is that you are up and ready to go again. It's a full-time job, believing in yourself. Carry this wherever you go, and you will never fall again, or even if you do, you will get up with a smile. Promise yourself that no matter how hard it gets, you won't give up.

When I fell, I didn't look around, but there were people looking at me. Some were happy, some unhappy, some wondering, some taking advantage, and yet some fell down with me to be able to feel what I felt and help me rise. Very seldom do you meet people who help you carry the cross and bleed with you. But if you have faith, then He who never left your side stays and looks after you forever. You need to find yourself in a world surrounded by people who wait to see you fall. As long as you have yourself, nothing else matters. Find yourself; you are more than enough. Every day I try to remember that the life I have now was something I prayed for always. Even with all the challenges and confusion, I asked to get this far. I wished for all this to happen.

The soul says, "Just in case no one told you this lately, you've done a great job in holding on to yourself through these difficult times. I am proud of you."

Finally, remember, whatever is true, whatever is noble, whatever is right, whatever is pure, whatever is lovely, whatever is admirable, if anything is excellent and praiseworthy, it's You. I survived saying this to my children and also to me; I needed it most.

I learned to say NO and set my priorities right. I followed my inner voice, stayed with whoever saw me grow, and loved me unconditionally. I built a new life for myself, and all those who helped me in my moment of truth stayed with me forever. "Happiness often sneaks in through a door you didn't know you left open." No matter if he or she had his or her own family or work or life, the little moments of support shown that changed my life stayed with me and were never forgotten. I will remain thankful forever.

Giving love without expecting anything in return is extremely courageous. If someone cannot reciprocate love, it's their issue, not a reflection of someone's worthiness. So be proud of your courage to love and be assured that the love you give will come back in some form.

There was a moment in my life when I felt I didn't exist at all. Every time I said or did something, it was proved wrong; I was made to feel unworthy of everything and for no reason. I looked for a different life where I would fit in and start again, but it left me broken and lost. It wasn't me, so I decided to return to my old world where I was made to feel unworthy, suppressed, unwanted, and prove who I was. Here I rebuilt my own world, fighting the odds because I knew what my value was. They were the toughest days of my life as I was trying to get back to who I always was by fighting against who I was made to be. My beliefs and faith got me back, and I never turned around after that.

Always pray to have eyes that see the best in people, a heart that forgives the worst, a mind that forgets the bad, and a soul that never loses faith.

God didn't remove the Red Sea. He parted it and made a way. Sometimes God doesn't remove our problems but shows us a way to pass through them. He gives us the strength, courage, and wisdom to traverse through the difficulties. Trust your instinct to show you the way. Let your heart be your guide.

The strongest people are the ones who are still kind after the world tore them apart.

Years passed, and I got my old self back. I was much stronger than before, and I knew I had to survive now that the storm was gone. New challenges, new hopes, and amidst everything, all I needed was an anchor for my restless mind. I still held strong to all the lessons learned all along my path and found peace in the truth. Every time I reminded myself that I went through more difficult times, and this will pass too. If you feel like you have lost something, remember that trees lose their leaves every year, yet they still stand tall and wait for better days to come. I accepted what happened. It was time to let go and move forward without living in a fantasy of what could have been, should have been, and would have been. I learned that "it did not work out" is NOT the same as "It will never work out." If I had to advise someone on a matter similar to mine, I would ask them to find love again. Everyone deserves a second chance, and love will find you someday if that's what you want.

All you need to do is leave your past behind, your past that broke you and doesn't let you move ahead. Remind yourself that it's a fresh start, a new chance for you that you should not let go of.

Leave your feelings aside and train your mind to be stronger than your feelings, or else you will lose yourself. Very soon, you will be surprised at how everything will miraculously work in your favour. You will realise that your current situation was only leading you to a blessing.

MOMENTS

I passed the hardest moment alone while everybody believed I was fine.

As a child, I grew up being the best player, the best runner, the most courageous girl, to become a commercial pilot, the decision-maker, the one who fights for others, the one who stood up against an abusive husband, the single mother who raised her kids singlehandedly, and the life coach who always put others ahead. It was a world where I was looked upon and adored by people who came my way. Even if I broke down sometimes, it was taken as a lesson learned by others. My life became a moment everyone looked forward to learning something from, and somewhere this made me a more positive and stronger person. I realised that I had nothing to contribute, but still, there was so much to give and make a difference to others by just being me. I was proud of myself that despite all the darkness I went through, I still chose to heal and shine. I went through the hardest moments alone, in tears that only made me tougher to face every situation.

Mom had said, "The ruthless will vanish, and the mockers will disappear, and those who are clean-hearted will sustain the test of time." I miss mom; writing about her itself leaves me teary-eyed. She knew me so well; she could see ahead of me, and I never considered that as a blessing when she was there. But now, I realise that everything she would say will happen, has always happened. It was always me who couldn't understand what destiny was trying to show me. On my darkest days, when I feel inadequate, unloved, and unworthy, I remember whose daughter I am, and I pull myself up.

Be true, be free, be you! This is what I was, and it was a gift from mom. Things happen in life, but was it a coincidence that after I went through hell I could still manifest with a clear mind and see what was coming? My thoughts were clear with no manipulation; I could see far before things would happen. This became a worry to some people, and some people swore by it. It was a transparent world where everything was seen through the visions and vibes that kept coming. I heard voices that said, "Don't worry about the people I removed from your life. I heard the conversation you didn't; I saw the things you couldn't and made moves you wouldn't."

It might look strange, but when I look back at the friends who remained friends and stood by me when I really needed them, there were very few; actually, only two. But that was more than enough; they were my two rocks, and I owe everything to them. Till today, they are by my side, and it is rare to find someone who cares about you without an agenda. One who wants to see you achieve your dreams, encourages you to grow and is there through all your mess. Such people were my two rocks, and I will always be grateful to them. I had countless friends, but most of them strayed away during my hard times or when the truth prevailed. I never looked back at people who left my side; I was okay with their decision. After all, a clean life matters more than a fake one. People don't care for you when you are alone; they just care for you when they are alone.

It's easy to judge others and more difficult to understand. Understanding needs compassion, patience, and a willingness to believe that good hearts don't change and sometimes deserve more support. People change sides; they all do for some reason, maybe to stay loyal to their spouses more than their friends, or maybe they felt they would have had to support me if they stayed, or maybe their loyalty lies with the male gender because they come across as stronger. But they forget that it all comes back. That's why after the betrayal, they all called for forgiveness and gave many excuses to avoid karma. But they forget that once it's done, nothing can undo it if it hurts the soul. That's why they say never hurt someone knowingly because it follows you and everyone attached to you till the end. God removes people from your life because he heard conversations and saw things happen that you didn't.

If someone forgives you from the heart, it's a different thing; part of it goes away. But if you are the cause of someone's pain, then you have to repent for the rest of your life.

There was an instance when I was harassed a lot in court during my separation; it was not fair as I was only seeking justice. The mental torture I was put through was very high for something little that I was asking for my kids. I told myself this world has no place for the truth, and however much you stay positive, somewhere it breaks you down. After a chanting and meditation session, I got a vision that I was standing high above the church stairs, praying, and the man came to hit me. At that time, I bent backward, and he missed hitting me and instead lost his balance, falling down the stairs into a ditch filled with black muck. He emerged from the ditch black in colour and screamed that he would get back at me. The next day in court, he lost custody of both the children but ended up not giving any alimony for their upbringing and needs. He thought he had won by refusing a livelihood for the kids, but instead, he had lost them forever.

Sometimes what didn't work out for you, in fact, worked out for you. I walked out happily; I had the children. God gave me the most valuable thing in the world, and at that time, all I could think about was how to give them a good life. The man thought that by refusing alimony for the kids and remarrying, he had it all, but eventually, he came back begging to see the kids he had given up. It was too late by then. God has his own way of showing things and teaching lessons. If we abide by it, it only clears our path. If we don't, then our path will only be filled with muck, just like the vision.

When I had a housewarming party in my new home, something didn't feel right at all. All his friends who were there couldn't look me in the eye, and even his family refused to confront me. Later, I came to know that they were hiding his affairs and keeping it a secret from me, knowing that he was cheating, I was going through a rough patch, and my children were also getting affected. Everyone there had a family too, but they forgot. It is only when it comes upon them that they realise the pain and betrayal that comes with infidelity. It was disheartening to witness their hypocrisy and lack of empathy, especially considering the impact it had on my kids. It made me question their morals and values as they seemed to prioritise their own interests over the well-being of others. It was a difficult time for me, but I knew I had to stay strong for my children and find a way to heal from the pain and betrayal.

I must have moved on, leaving the past behind, but I will not forgive the hurt caused. I went through sleepless nights, and the level of pain my kids went through was immense. I am a healer; I have forgotten the past, but the universe hasn't, and it will come back to everyone the same way, if not now, then in the next generation. I have the patience to wait and see all that will be shown to me.

The giver also needs to receive, the healer also needs healing, the planner also needs surprises, the thoughtful also needs to be thought of, the considerate also needs to be considered, and it is not how much you have learned but how much you have absorbed in what you have learned. At a young age, there was nothing more left to learn but to give away all that I learned so that life somewhere becomes easier for others.

My story is filled with broken pieces, terrible choices, and ugly truths. It's also filled with a major comeback, peace in my soul, and a grace that saved my life. I would tell myself every day, "I am better than yesterday, I love my life, and I love my children. I have to do everything alone. I am a mother and a father too. I am not perfect; I make mistakes, forget things, lose my cool, and some days I go a little crazy too. But it is okay because in the end, no one could love my children the way I do."

People don't abandon the people they love; they abandon the people they are using, and that's all the closure I needed.

THE COURT

When my lawyer heard me out, she said it was a matter of abuse. Until then, I was told that it was a common thing that happens in all families. I started collecting documents and pictures and recalling instances to support my case. I was told that the more points I had, the stronger the case would be in front of the judge.

At this point, I had a marathon planned in Leh, and I told my lawyer I would come back with the papers ready. I left for Leh four days before the marathon just to find time to meditate and finish my court papers. Every morning after a practice run, I would go to a monastery and meditate. After that, I would sit somewhere in a quiet location and start writing. This continued for a few days, and I put down seventy-five instances of physical and mental abuse. This sounds easy, but the whole time I was writing, I was in a trance. I had to reimagine the incidents and put it in writing, and every time I was doing so, the same thing kept repeating and repeating. I had sleepless nights and wept for hours. I stepped out in the evenings to meet my friends Tenzing and Pema in the main market. They had a shop there, and whenever they saw me, they would get me something to eat, knowing that that was the only time I stepped out. Tenzing would drop me off at a monastery every morning pick me up later and drop me back to my room. He knew something was not good with me, but I always said I was missing the kids. My papers were ready, but I became very stressed with all that was going on and couldn't complete my Khardungla run. I gave up in the last seven kilometres, feeling nauseous. Nevertheless, I bid goodbye to Leh and returned with a Blue Tara, who was my inspiration throughout my stay and meditations. I learned to chant to her in the monasteries. I sat for hours looking for answers. She answered all my thoughts and made sure I came back with a clear mind, knowing that it was the right thing to do.

I learned the power of chanting and continued until today as it brings me a sense of calm and clarity. It has become a part of my daily routine, helping me stay focused and centred amidst the chaos of everyday life. The repetitive nature of chanting can help quiet the mind and body, promoting a state of relaxation. This can be especially helpful for people who are dealing with stress, anxiety, or other mental health conditions. Chanting can also help boost mood and reduce negative emotions. This is likely due to the release of endorphins, which are hormones that have mood-boosting effects.

Improves focus and concentration. When we chant, we focus on the sound of the prayer and the rhythm of our breath. This can help improve focus and concentration, which can be beneficial for concentrating on a task.

Increases self-awareness. Chanting can help us become more aware of our thoughts, feelings, and bodily sensations. This can be especially helpful for people who feel isolated or alone. In many cultures, chanting is seen as a way to connect with the divine or a higher power. This can be a source of comfort and strength during a difficult period.

My strength at a time when I was all alone was Tara. She is the eye of wisdom and protection in Tibetan Buddhism. The Blue Tara is believed to have powers to eliminate obstacles, negative energy, and harmful influences from our lives. In addition to her protective nature, she is believed to have healing powers, and her teachings continue to inspire and transform individuals worldwide. The first thing I did after I returned from Leh was get a tattoo of Tara.

I filed my papers in the domestic violence court and got a date for the first hearing. Upon knowing that there was chaos in the house, I was called names and labelled a homewrecker, making my life miserable. I requested a separation and asked him to move to our new house, but he refused, saying that he would not go anywhere until he threw me out on the streets. This continued for a while and was affecting the children too. One evening, in a drunken state, he was instigating me with his mobile phone, and as I ran inside the room and closed the door, my hand came in-between, and my two right fingers got injured. I never felt the pain, though the floor was full of blood. He kept telling me to go to the hospital, but I refused. In the end, when I realised I might lose my hand due to severe bleeding, I called my friend who lives downstairs. I made it clear that he would leave the house before harming me more, or else I would call the police. After my injury was reported, he received a restraining order from the court until the judgment was passed.

My case moved to the family court as he refused to pay any alimony, and the lawyer said that the next step was to file for a divorce. By then, the man had happily moved into the new house with his new girlfriend. This new house was in a posh building and was registered in my name as my dad had also paid for it. He also ensured that if the house was in my name, there would be an additional discount given. I waited for the building to get ready and started doing the interior work to move in. Every day I would visit the house and sit with the workers doing the work. The hall, kitchen, baths, cupboards, and electricals – but in the end, he moved in with someone else. I accepted everything, believing that whatever happens is for the good, and better days await me.

The court days were the most stressful; the timings were odd, and we had to wait all day sometimes for the judge. Things would take a turn without me knowing, and sometimes I had to sit in the same room with him for hours. He had a fancy lawyer who would always come dressed up. I had refused to talk to her from day one because she had called me a girl with loose character in front of the judge. I answered her, saying that it was he who lived with his girlfriend in my house, whereas I lived with my kids. Hearing this, I saw her asking him if it was true, and he had no answer. But later, I started saying hello to her because I realised that courtrooms are made to put a person's morale down, so I didn't bother much after that. Later, when everything was over, she came to me and apologised, which was quite touching. She said she regretted everything she said about me and that a wrong decision was made from his side. She also added that I should get back to work to support the kids and that the decision made by her client was wrong, and he would regret it. Again, I only said, "God watches over us, and I need not worry."

The family court finally granted us a divorce and gave me custody of both my children. This was the biggest joy in my life; I was finally free, and both my kids were going to be with me, and he had no rights over them because he refused to pay alimony. But he would still be paying all their education expenses till the end.

I kept the house and gave him the new house. I said to myself, "As long as my children are with me, I don't need anything else. I will work to make ends meet and keep us together and rocking till the end. We love our life now; there is no one to harass us either drunk or fighting or something else. Everything is quiet and peaceful."

LIFE IS A WONDERFUL THING

"'Hate' has three letters but so does 'love',

'Enemies' has seven letters but so does 'friends'

'Lying' has five letters but so does 'truth',

'Cry' has three letters but so does 'joy',

'Negativity' has ten letters but so does 'positivity',

Life is two-sided, choose the better side of it."

The many instances that bring back a smile are full in my life; I try to make moments simple and light-hearted for all so that everyone gets to keep a part of it. Life, as they say, always gives you back what you put in. So, for me, it was love and compassion, my everything.

When I was small, I used to love distributing goodies to everyone just to make them happy and smile. Most of the time, it was to my tenants and neighbours, mostly on special occasions. Also, because we had a huge garden of fruits and vegetables, every time they were harvested, the kitchen used to be filled with bags of fruits and veggies. I loved taking the bags that mom packed to everyone's house. In return, I always received a chocolate or something else. Special occasions were Eid, birthdays, promotions, Christmas, exam passes, etc. Dad always said we must share and relish whatever God provides.

The many directions that life showed me and the many that I followed only reminded me of people all along who contributed to what I am today. Whenever something ends, something better starts, which is why I never get scared of starting new, also because I have nothing to lose. I know that God provides, and he never fails all those who believe in his presence.

In the meantime, my life took off in a direction I never imagined. My hobbies turned into a successful career that brought me fulfilment and joy. I never anticipated that something I loved doing for fun would become my means of making a living and pursuing my passion.

A healthy lifestyle that I always followed is what inspired me to turn my hobbies into a career. By prioritising a fitter mind and body, I realised the importance of doing what truly brings me happiness. This realisation motivated me to take a leap of faith and transform my hobbies into a successful profession. As I continue to thrive in my chosen path, I am grateful for the unexpected turn my life took, as it has allowed me to not only find personal fulfilment but also inspire and positively impact those around me. To me, what was most important was to find work within what was already in me. I didn't have to struggle to find a job because I knew my strengths and passions. Instead, I focused on honing my skills to discover opportunities that aligned with my interests. This approach allowed me to pursue a fulfilling career that brought out the best in me and brought me happiness.

There were very few people as fit as dad; whatever his schedule might be, the one thing he would never miss was his morning walks and stretches. Even during his last few days, he was out with a walking stick until he could manage.

My early morning routine came from dad as he would drag me every morning with him for walks, which turned into runs and finally stayed with me forever. As a child, dad had kept a personal trainer for me. Every morning, we used to gather at my gate and start our runs and then work out at the local ground, and then jog back home. Those were the strongest days of my life, and I held onto them as my pillars of strength. As I grew up, my days would be gloomy and dull without a morning jog and a few exercises. The way my day would be depended on a strong morning workout. I lived all my life following the same routine wherever I was and in whatever condition or situation. It also became my soulmate and my companion. I would confront my sorrows and my happiness in it; I would also talk and pour out my heart, which I wouldn't let out to anyone else. My life was an open page and could be read by no one but my runs. They saw my weaker side of loneliness and betrayal and strengthened me. They showed me the right path by clearing my mind of thoughts that blocked it. They kept boosting me and were my source of positive thoughts. They aroused a happy feeling by constantly making my heart pump more so that the negative is pumped out and the positive is sucked in. They became my bestie after I realised what they did for me, and I never wanted to stay away from them. My worst moments were turned to calmness, and it opened ways for me to decide what was good for me. It was my moment of solitude, which was a gift from Dad, and I realised it only after I lost him.

Many people did not relate to my affinity for a healthy mind and body that I had since childhood, as most people begin living healthier lifestyles much later in life after a late realisation. But for me, this is always who I was, and perhaps that's why I always had a friend in me to turn to any time I needed one.

I was in the middle of a crossroads when my marriage ended, and I won the custody battle for my children. This is what I was fighting for all this time and was going through a rough patch, but finally, I won and was given sole custody of the children. My prayers were answered, and all I needed now was a stable income to make sure the kids didn't feel any change in their lifestyle and accept that I was both parents to them now.

This was a tough one for me as all these years after I stopped flying, I never took up another job except being a full-time mother to my kids. My days would start and end with the kids, and I never saw the need to work, as I never thought one day I would be on my own looking after the children. But destiny was different here. I was racking my brains thinking about what I could do or what I was good at that would fetch me some income. I tried many avenues but all in vain; no one needed someone like me who wasn't qualified for anything except flying an airplane. That too, with the long break, it was impossible to get back to flying now. It was possible with a long training schedule, which meant leaving the kids and home behind for long periods and concentrating only on training. I had to make up my mind and set my priorities right as I was the sole decision-maker here, and there was no backup.

This was a huge moment for me because my kids were my whole world. I knew they needed me more than anything, especially since I noticed some people acting differently, and it made them feel insecure. Being a single parent with no family around, they had no one else to turn to. I had to protect them and help them rebuild their lives after the separation. Finding work was important too, but my main focus was on the kids. I had to find a balance between giving them all my energy and finding a job that would allow me to do so. Courage isn't always loud; sometimes it's just a quiet voice at the end of the day saying, "I will try again tomorrow."

I stayed calm, knowing that the storm would eventually pass and things would get better. My strength became my saviour, and I found my answer. It was like my dad was guiding me towards a path that was already there, but I just couldn't see it because I was looking in the wrong places for answers. During this time, the training groups I had for marathon training and exercises boomed up, and I started taking workouts and teaching about a healthy and fit lifestyle, receiving lots of good feedback. It all started with friends getting together for runs, and the group getting bigger; then we gave a name to the group, and it kept growing. All it took was experience and knowledge about what I was good at, and it all fell into place. People started liking what I did and joined me for workouts. I got a few certifications and started training professionally, and it all worked out as I didn't have to do much to qualify as a trainer because I was a runner and a fitness enthusiast from childhood. I never stopped; it all fell into place. The calf muscles that I developed as a child carried me a long way; they stayed most loyal to me as all my work involved physical activity and strength building, and they were my two pillars.

Additionally, I began therapy and healing sessions. It all began with my non-profit organisation, where I worked tirelessly to get homeless people off the streets and provide them with access to housing and basic necessities. I gave them advice on putting their families first and quitting harmful behaviours. I also sought to help them find jobs and provide for their children's education so that they could live in homes with the money they earned each day, rather than on the streets. This gave me an immense sense of fulfilment and began my path as a healer. I enjoyed contributing to the well-being of others because I felt like I was benefiting myself. I recognised myself in those who sought my help, and when they were settled, I felt content.

I started training in the mornings and managed my NGO during the day. I made time to be home whenever the kids got back from their classes, and I was there for them in school, college, outings, picking and dropping them until they became independent and needed me less for all these trips. But I still continued because, for me, being there was most important. The end result is that whatever I did while growing up stayed with me until the end. This is how I survived when the need arose, and this is how it became my strength for the rest of my life.

I thank my dad for somehow knowing that someday all that I would need would be the wisdom he left behind. When he was there, it never occurred to me how important every word he said was, but after he was gone, everything made sense and everything mattered. How I wish I had heard more and learned more, but nevertheless, he watches over me and reminds me every day that he is there and never left me.

With everything my parents left behind for me, there was a house too; it was our ancestral house in Guwahati, Assam. All I knew was that when I was struggling with my court cases and supporting my kids singlehandedly, the only asset I had was the money the house fetched me after getting sold. This, again, I felt was kept for me for my dire straits moment, and it was somehow known to them. Every parent wants the best for their children even after they are no more, but I feel my parents never left me before making sure I would be fine even if I had to manage everything alone.

No matter how hard someone tried to break me, I somehow managed to stay strong. I stood my ground like a rock because I knew what was coming, and I was prepared. I had been shown the path ahead, so whatever happened, my reaction was like "I've seen this before." I saw things as signs, whether they came to me in visions or even dreams. I became more and more aware that even during those tough times, someone was watching over me. They never left my side, and sometimes I could feel their presence. They communicated with me through vibes and intuitions.

I prayed and thanked them, promising to make the world a better place for those who cared for me, just as they did. I also wanted to create a better future for my children, who now only have me as both parents. I kept my promise by never saying no to my kids for something I could afford. And just like my loyal friends who never abandoned me, I never left their side either. I stayed true to them in times of need and pain, always putting them and their loved ones before myself.

There are apologies you will never get and words you deserve to hear that will never come. There are conversations you'll never have and questions that will never be answered. There are quick explanations that if they had offered, could have saved a lifetime of believing you did something wrong. And you could spend your whole life replaying events over and over again, wondering if it was you. But it wasn't you. It was never you. And I hope that you know you are so much more than how they made you feel. How they treated you was never a reflection of your own worth. You're worth the peace you cultivate from letting go of what no longer serves you. You're worth the love that blooms within you as you reconnect with your deepest self. You're worth the joy you rediscover and the fulfilment you find from people and places and experiences that nourish your soul. You're worth new beginnings. You're worth being enchanted by life again. Don't let anyone take that away from you.

RUNNING

2837

When I was a child, my convent school was on top of a hill where only a cross could be seen from afar. I was always dropped off and picked up from school, and I would always admire the kids who would walk to school, chit-chatting. I tried it and realised how difficult it was. The route was a steep climb and required a lot of energy to reach school, although coming down was easy. Years after I passed out of school, I covered this climb and other climbs in my morning run. It became an everyday habit for me, which I never missed. There was a statue of Mother Mary in the school where I would stop for a prayer and then return.

On a few mornings when I felt like doing a longer run, I would go to Jotsoma. That was again a long, tedious route. I had done my twelfth there in the science college and was familiar with the terrain. There were waterfalls and thick jungles throughout the route, and you could only hear the birds and bees. Jotsoma is an Angami village located about ten kilometres from Kohima. In those days, completing this run was a big task, but what I am today is all because of what I developed in my initial days of running.

A morning run in the hills, full of trees and flowers, is where I initially learned to run. It was so refreshing to breathe in the fresh air and feel the morning chills. I started my run early in the morning when the air was still cool and crisp. I would follow the same trail every morning through the hills, past towering trees and colourful wildflowers. As I ran, I would listen to the sounds of the birds chirping and the wind rustling through the leaves, the rooster crowing, and the smell of the first kitchen fire. I would feel the sun on my face and the breeze in my hair.

By the time I finished my run, I felt refreshed and invigorated. I had a sense of peace and well-being that would last all day.

On my way back, I would meet dad somewhere stretching or meeting up with an old friend. The only question asked would be, "How much did you run?"

Dad was an early morning person, healthy, strong, tall, very positive, and would never miss his morning walks, no matter how cold the morning was. When he initially started taking me with him in the mornings, it was as a companion, but later, I left him behind and started running ahead. We started taking loops where we would bump into each other after every loop. When that got boring, I started taking longer loops where we wouldn't see each other. This scared him when he wouldn't see me in the thick morning fog, and he would ask every passerby if they crossed me. To satisfy himself, he kept a coach for me, a Bengali football coach from Mohun Bagan. Dad gave him a place to stay in our building and made him train all the kids in the building in his free time and take me for runs in the mornings. This worked out well; I became a better and faster runner with the correct form. I would do strength training and stretching with him, and my runs became longer. The one person who was enjoying all this was dad. He would always try to find new ways to keep me going, thinking that I might get bored and stop. But I never did, wherever I was, I would always talk to dad about where and how much I ran and my progress.

At 17, I left for the US to become a pilot, and my runs were on open roads and in parks. It was hot compared to Kohima; my heart rate was always high, and I was dehydrated most of the time. Texas didn't have those cool running temperatures. My mileage stayed low but regular. Early morning runs became difficult as my flying schedule was also early morning. I shifted to evening runs, and it stayed that way for a long time. But I remember drinking gallons of water during my runs in the hot, humid evening weather. It was different compared to my normal runs, with many changes in the pattern due to my flying schedule, but I continued as I had promised dad not to stop. Then came Italy and the Alps where I stayed for four years, with the same weather as when I first started running: cold, crisp early morning air biting your cheeks. Here I ran by the lake and small alleys. I got back to my normal morning routine. I had a lot of free time, so my runs were never missed. I started doing longer runs and terrains.

Familiar weather and a sporty spirit compared to the US. I learned to cycle too but didn't take it up seriously as I liked running more. I would go to live in the Alps for days on my own where I would run up and down the snow mountains just to get a kick out of it. Here I would see the Italian football teams practicing, so I would get more pepped up. Listening to their loud singing during the practice made me homesick. The only thing you could feel in these runs were your cold cheeks; all the rest were happy and numb. Many places to run and memories to cherish.

Then came Mumbai after I got a job at Jet Airways. New city, new surroundings; I would travel far for my runs. Jogger's Park Bandra and PDP were better places to run, other than Juhu beach, the University campus, Don Bosco, etc. Hot weather makes it impossible to run during the day. There were very few runners; I would hardly see people running. My colleagues had never run in their entire lives, and they thought I was crazy to run so much. The morning crowd were not runners, and the culture of early morning long runs didn't exist. I looked for groups to run with and marathons to participate in, but there were none. There was a vast difference between running in a group abroad and here. People were not very disciplined in running; they never took it casually. For some time, I was posted in Delhi and had a house in Defence Colony. There was a long nala that stretched from the start to the end of Defence Colony, and that was my running route every day. I would go round and round the nala. One thing I learned about running in Delhi: "Do not run after sunrise." Hope you understand what I mean by that. I was also warned but didn't believe it until I was touched by a passing car. I started going to parks and gardens for runs where no one could lay hands on you and drive off.

I was back in Mumbai and followed the same routine: beach run, and park run until I met Dan. He was a running coach and trained runners at NRC. I decided to train under him to refine my runs. He would provide me with a training schedule to follow, and I had to update him every day. I felt at ease now, and I also became good friends with Dan. It became a routine to do our Sunday runs together. I learned one thing during that time that I still advise people because it worked for me: Run long and fast on Saturday and on Sunday, run with tired legs, slower and longer. That's the best way to build leg strength. Running became more interesting as I started running marathons. It was a significant accomplishment for people to run marathons; they prepared for months to complete it in a good time. SCMM was the biggest craze, and it felt nice to see so many runners. My first SCMM bib was a gift from my coach, and I still have it. After that, I trained hard to achieve better runs. I did a few sub-two-hour half marathons and then shifted to full marathons and ultra-marathons. These required more practice for endurance buildup, and the only days I could dedicate to long practice runs were Sundays because of the kids. Sometimes, even that was not possible due to other obligations at home. I didn't receive much support for my runs; many times, I was told that I was dedicating all my time to running and neglecting the kids and home. It happened every time I went for a run. I would tell myself that I had waited for this for so long, and now, when I have it, it is so easily taken away.

Despite all the time constraints for training, I managed to progress from a half marathon to a full marathon to a seventy-five-kilometre ultra marathon within a year. The next year, I ran a hundred kilometres and achieved a podium finish. A lot of credit goes to Dan, who pushed me physically and mentally, especially since I lost my Dad and Mom during those days. The rest of the credit goes to my physical strength since childhood which stayed with me throughout. It was actually my grit to carry on; I could have given up, but I didn't. I didn't have much to fall back on. My runs became my companion. I found peace in running, and it was my most significant stress buster.

I did many more full marathons and ultras after that. In total, thirty-two half marathons, sixteen full marathons, and seven ultras. If you were to ask me what I achieved from all this, I would say I found a world away from all the pain and suffering. Although the runs were painful, I realised they took away all the sorrows I was going through at that time. Sometimes it was an excuse to get away, and I wished never to leave that zone. Even though I didn't have much time for long practice runs, I managed to finish all my runs only because my foundation was strong.

The number of marathons increased, and so did the number of runners. Many people took it up as a passion and as a competitive sport. It changed the way people felt about healthy habits and staying fit. It created awareness for a good cause, which wasn't there before. It was flooded with runners all over social media, every corner of parks, roads, clubs, gyms, etc. Lots of flaunting too. It was a good thing that running had meaning now. All this and many more, but for me, running still remained the same as it was when I started. Listen to your body, all I needed was a bottle of water and shoes to run in, and the road was mine. Eventually, you run for yourself.

When I started running less to give time to my other priorities, I started focusing more on fitness and a healthy lifestyle. This was always my goal; I was giving more emphasis on living healthily and strongly. I started taking sessions for running and fitness. My group was called Running Buddies. I had trainers who trained people in different locations. The main focus was running and strength training. I got a few certifications done and started training in my free time. Soon my training picked up, and I started training in different locations and online. I didn't have to work too hard to train; it came naturally, and I was enjoying it.

Along with training, I started organising runs for my group. The next step was our own marathons since we were a big group. Two marathons a year in different locations. It was fun. I made sure that in every marathon I organised, there was a special guest list of runners who were there in my initial days of running. This was a way to show my respect to them.

Whenever something good happens, some people try to pull you down. On many occasions, things didn't go smoothly because of people not wanting to see me do well in what they wanted most. But the difference was that I had it in me all my life, while others were struggling to achieve it. Many brands came with false promises for their temporary benefit. They get what they want and leave. The common thing that they all want is visibility without wanting to do the heavy lifting. I never held on to any of them. Later, I decided I was my own brand and didn't need any other collaborations.

There was only one brand that remained authentic throughout the course of many years, developing expertise in this area. Their sole goal was to create a fitter and healthier community. To achieve this, they were willing to open all possible doors. I'll never forget my initial encounter with Infiniti Mall and with Gaurav and Rahul. They were shining examples of optimism, and they never rejected anything I had said. I came to understand that everything works out when two individuals have the same ideas and attempt to work things out for the good of others. A Fitter Body and Mind was something we wanted to bring to light. From that time until today, their gates are open to anyone who wants to stay fit and healthy. I take workouts here with my trainers, and there is always a good response, which means all my hard work of making people believe in a Fit Body and Mind worked.

I promote a healthy lifestyle, something we all need. It can be a combination of any physical activity and a healthy way of living through wellness and a balanced diet. When everyone had settled on something for themselves, I settled on promoting the physical and mental well-being of people around me.

Fall in love with your life.

Wake up early. Meditate. Connect with your mind. Be kind to yourself in the mirror. Wear an outfit that makes you feel good. Do any physical activity for over forty-five minutes. Elevate your senses. Go for a run, a walk, a swim, a cycle, or yoga. Stretch. Breathe deeply. Spend time working on your passion. Eat your favourite food. Show yourself gratitude. Engage in activities that bring you joy and make you feel alive. Surround yourself with positive and supportive people who uplift and inspire you. Take time to nourish your body with nutritious meals and hydrate yourself adequately throughout the day. Prioritise self-care and make time for relaxation and rejuvenation. Remember, loving your life starts with loving yourself first.

When starting a new fitness routine, it is important to prioritise activities that you are familiar with and that align with your current fitness level. Engaging in unfamiliar or physically demanding activities without proper guidance can increase the risk of injury. Remember, it's better to focus on consistency and gradually incorporate new activities as you build strength and endurance.

Do what's right for your body's strength without exceeding its limit. Pushing your body beyond its limits can lead to burnout and potential setbacks in your fitness journey. It's essential to listen to your body and give it the rest it needs to recover and adapt.

By maintaining consistency and gradually challenging yourself, you can achieve long-term success in achieving your fitness goals.

Be a part of my group that guides you towards what's best for you by providing support and motivation along the way. Surrounding yourself with like-minded individuals can help keep you accountable and make the journey more enjoyable. Together, you can explore new activities and find what works best for each individual's unique strengths and abilities. Find your fit here and discover a community that celebrates progress and encourages personal growth. With our diverse range of fitness options and expert guidance, you'll have the opportunity to try different workouts and discover what truly resonates with you. Join us and embark on a transformative journey towards a healthier, happier you.

These days, everyone only pushes for a timing during marathons, ignoring their body's potential, which can lead to injury. It is crucial to recognise that focusing solely on achieving specific timings during marathons can often overshadow the importance of listening to our bodies. Neglecting our body's potential and pushing beyond its limits can result in serious injuries. Therefore, it is essential to strike a balance between setting goals and prioritising our overall well-being to ensure a safe and enjoyable marathon experience. Listen to your body and do not get carried away by people who may be running at a faster pace. Each individual has their own unique abilities and limitations, and it's important to honour those boundaries to prevent any potential harm. Remember, the ultimate goal is not just to cross the finish line, but to maintain a healthy and sustainable approach to running for long-term fitness and well-being. The key to a good marathon is proper training and preparation. This includes gradually increasing your mileage, incorporating strength and cross-training exercises, and following a balanced nutrition plan. Additionally, it's crucial to stay hydrated during the race and fuel your body with the right amount of carbohydrates for energy. By taking these steps, you can ensure that you are physically and mentally prepared for the demands of a marathon, increasing your chances of a successful and enjoyable experience.

Give family obligations priority over other activities. Strive to strike a balance between your personal and training time. You won't find serenity or be able to proceed until you realise this. Try to maintain a healthy work-life balance. By allocating specific time slots for each aspect of your life, you can ensure that you are dedicating enough time to your family, completing your work responsibilities efficiently, and engaging in regular physical activities. This will not only help you stay physically fit but also improve your mental well-being and overall productivity. Recovery time from any activity is most important as it allows your body and mind to rest and rejuvenate. It is crucial to schedule adequate recovery time in your daily routine to prevent burnout and promote optimal performance in all areas of your life. Remember, taking care of yourself is just as important as taking care of your other commitments. Meditate and energise your mind through mindfulness practices or engaging in activities that bring you joy and relaxation. By incorporating moments of stillness and reflection into your routine, you can reduce stress and enhance your mental clarity. Additionally, make sure to prioritise quality sleep as it plays a vital role in restoring your body and mind, allowing you to wake up refreshed and ready to tackle the day ahead.

I'm going to write down some running guidance that I've always followed. I've evolved into who I am now by heeding these. I never gave up, neither physically nor mentally. Simple ways of living serve as a constant example for you.

1. Choose a distance that is appropriate for your fitness level. Wear comfortable running shoes and clothing. Perhaps shoes half a size larger, but not too tight. Try them on for a few small runs before wearing them for a long run. If you experience bruising or discomfort in your toes, avoid using them for extended runs. It's best to have your foot analysis done before purchasing shoes. This also saves you from the headache of ill-fitting shoes and helps you make informed choices every time.

2. A dry-fit t-shirt, vest, and shorts work best for any run. The material is quick-drying and won't chafe you from sweat. There's a wide range available from different brands; just be wise in your choices since they'll be used exclusively for your runs. The material is synthetic, which is not recommended for wearing throughout the day.

3. Start early in the morning when the air is cooler. Be aware of your surroundings. Always carry a bottle of electrolyte or water and a light if it's dark in the morning. Try to avoid using earphones in the dark, as you need to be more cautious.

4. Set a goal. What distance do you want to run? Once you know your goal, you can start planning your training and runs. Run sustainably. Don't try to do too much too soon. Start with shorter distances and gradually increase your mileage. Stress can take a toll on your physical and mental health, so it's important to find ways to manage it. For me, my runs were my stress busters; it was a way to relax and clear my mind. For many years, this worked for me; I would set out for a run, and my mood would change entirely.

5. Rest, recover, and sleep. This is essential for muscle repair and recovery. Ensure you're getting enough sleep each night.

6. Eat to fuel your body. Eating a healthy diet will give you the energy you need to train and race. Incorporate strength

training into your routine to build muscle and prevent injuries.

7. Eat and run. Ultra-marathons and full marathons can be long, so it's important to learn how to eat and drink during your run. Test what suits you before trying them for the first time during your long run. If it's not easily digested, your entire run will get ruined. Also, do not overeat, but make sure whatever you eat replenishes what your body has lost.

8. Be patient. It takes time to build up the endurance and strength needed for a long run. Don't get discouraged if you don't see results immediately.

9. Listen to your body. Don't push yourself too hard, or you'll risk injury. Take rest days when you need them; having someone to train with can help you stay motivated. Find a running buddy who can train with you.

With so much said about fitness, I really want to share my soul foods with you. It's something I have always loved, and it became my comfort food as I grew up. These are the healthiest and simplest of meals. They offer solace during stressful or depressing moments, as well as when you need some quiet time and rejuvenation. These easy meals have the ability to replenish both our bodies and our emotions. Whether it's Ghee Rice on a tired day or a soothing plate of Boiling Chicken and rice on a cold day, these meals hold a special place in my heart since they remind me of the love and warmth I experienced as a child. They are more than just meals because of how wholesome and simple they are. I would choose to come home without dining out to have my soul food in my comfort zone. The flavours and aromas transport me back to cherished memories, making it more than just a meal that brings me a sense of nostalgia and happiness. It's not just about the taste but also the emotional connection I have with these dishes. It's like a warm hug for my soul, providing comfort and satisfaction like no other food can. These dishes never fail to uplift my spirits and rejuvenate my tired mind. Their simplicity and familiarity bring a sense of ease and contentment, allowing me to unwind and recharge for whatever lies ahead.

Here's a list of some of my soul foods:

- Hot Rice with ghee and three boiled eggs
- Rice with Dal water and green chilli
- Rice with Chicken boiled with ginger and chilli
- Pasta with chilli and garlic
- Lettuce tomato cucumber chicken and egg salad
- Quinoa with broccoli and chicken
- Rice with fried fish
- Two apples

Many times I had to cook only for myself, as no one else enjoyed these meals. But to me, they still remain my soul food, and even though they taste different in different parts of the world, I would still come home to make myself one.

FAITH SAVE & CARE FOUNDATION

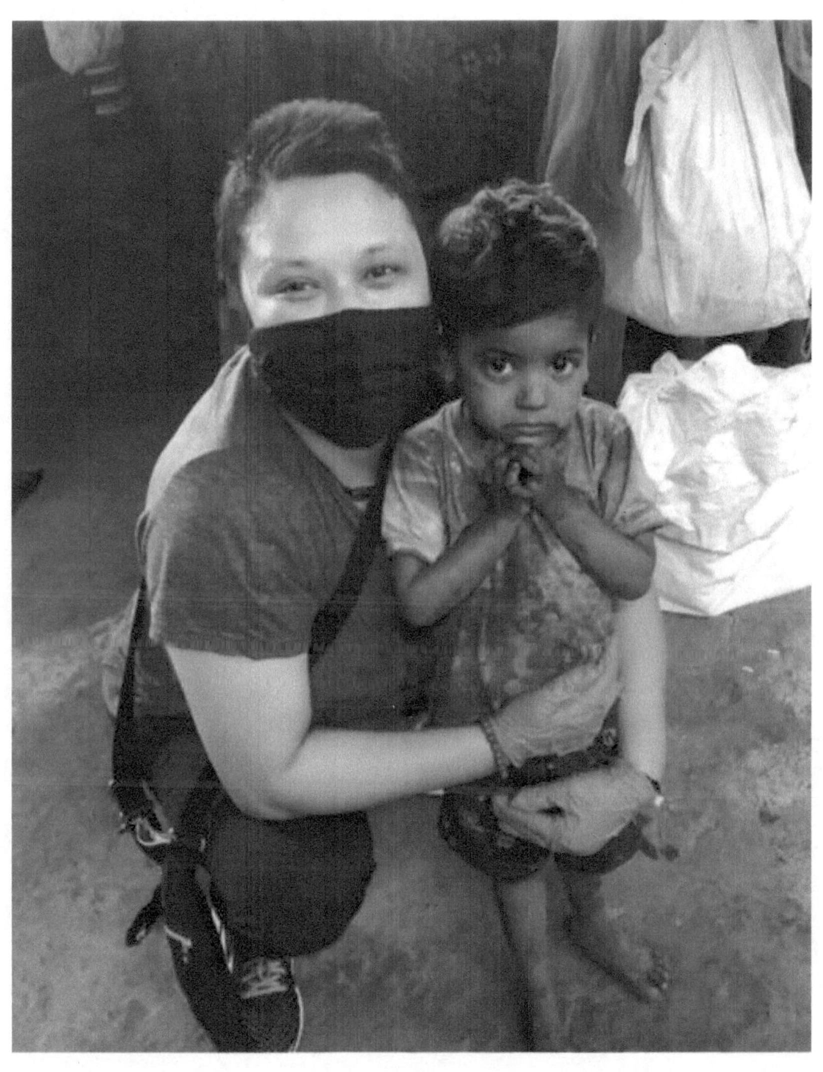

A single act of kindness can change someone's life. Be the reason someone smiles. Be a beacon of love in a world that often forgets to be. It doesn't take much to make a difference, whether it's offering a helping hand or simply listening with empathy. Small acts of kindness can have a profound impact on both the giver and the receiver, reminding us of our shared humanity. Let us be the aid to heal wounds, mend broken hearts, and bring hope to those who are struggling in a world that can sometimes feel cold and indifferent. So let us choose kindness, not only for the impact it has on others but also for the joy and fulfilment it brings to our own lives. Even the smallest act can have a profound impact on someone, reminding them that they are seen, valued, and loved. So let us give hope to the needy and create a world where compassion and empathy prevail.

Numerous events led me to become a lightworker and a philanthropist. It could have been realising I could change the world for the better after seeing the suffering of others who were less fortunate than I was. These things sparked a strong desire in me to devote my life to serving those around me, especially children. Maybe they were lessons for me that started at a young age, as I was raised in a family that valued compassion and empathy. Seeing my parents and grandparents actively involved in charitable work inspired me to follow in their footsteps and use my privilege to uplift those in need. This journey has taught me the importance of gratitude and the immense joy that comes from giving back to the needy.

The love for any fellow human being—to see them live just a little better and to provide them with a suitable living condition, be it by giving away part of what you have or by getting help from people equally wanting to provide for the same—is what gives the most happiness. This act of selflessness not only brings joy to the person being helped but also creates a sense of fulfilment and purpose in the giver's life. It fosters a deep connection between individuals and makes the world a more caring place.

The world sees the poor as a class of society to keep away from; many times they are avoided as unwanted things and as a burden, but one forgets that everyone comes to the world by the same creator; some are born rich and some are born poor, but again, when life ends, everyone goes back to the same creator. So, the lifespan in this world is only temporary; we come to be tested for a higher purpose, and once done, our lives start in a world where we exist according to our ability to serve the creator. In this temporary world, it is important to remember that our purpose extends beyond material wealth and societal judgements. Our true worth lies in how we use our abilities to contribute to the greater good and fulfill our spiritual responsibilities. Therefore, it is crucial to embrace compassion and empathy towards those who may be less fortunate, recognising that their circumstances do not define their inherent value as human beings.

Life in this world has multiple levels of performance to survive and reach a higher level if materialistic goals become the main need. The process leaves behind people who don't fit in, and in due course, they are left behind like scum and unwanted creatures. They are treated as a burden in society and are made to fetch for their survival through the lowest kind of work any human can do. These individuals often face extreme hardships and struggle to find a sense of purpose or belonging. They are forced to endure a life of constant struggle, lacking the opportunities and resources necessary to escape their circumstances. In this relentless pursuit of survival, individuals often find themselves trapped in a vicious cycle where the desperation to meet basic needs outweighs any sense of fulfilment or purpose. The struggle for survival becomes all-consuming, overshadowing the potential for personal growth and self-actualisation. There are those in the world who are unable to make ends meet; they struggle, they survive, and they carry on, but regardless of their own survival, they tend to find themselves worrying about the uncertainties of others. The gap between the wealthy and the poor may be incredibly unfair, making some people doubt their own existence while still inspiring others to dream big and work towards achieving it. The person who survives in all of this is the one who assists others on their journey; ultimately, the provider emerges above all others, not the richest person.

A philanthropist is someone who is compassionate towards the needy and tries to work towards giving them something more or better than what they have. She works to make others survive and live better than what they have; she provides them with their daily needs, shows them the path to success, and counsels them for the better.

The world needs people who live for others, not only because they have lived enough, but because they see the need in others, and fulfilling these needs becomes important. They do so not only through materialistic help but also emotionally and by connecting with them in other ways to heal their lives.

Many big organisations that call themselves help to the needy are only helping people get a salary in their organisation. They hire people and give them a salary to ask the world for help, but most of the help that comes goes for the upkeep of the organisation for their day-to-day work and paying salaries and bills. Very little goes for what they work for. Also, many misuse the funds for illegal work and to generate extra funds, but all for their own needs.

Actual field work is what these organisations need to be doing, but many times the misuse of funds tends to be so high that you wonder whether people have any conscience left. When the need for help arises, the need is for the distressed and not for your organisation's running needs. When disaster happens, all such organisations come alive, but it's all just to fulfill their own needs and not those of the needy.

Blessed are those who do good for others, make a change, help people survive, get their lives going, and make sure that distress is not the name of their workplace.

When the need arises and people use the need as an opportunity to extract and misuse it, then the need to end such acts becomes a higher need. We live in a world where humanity is valued lower because it generates no funds, but everything doesn't have to generate funds to have value. Humanity is the highest valued asset anyone can possess; it stays with you till the end, when all others leave you behind, including your own body parts. Humanity needs no investment but has the highest returns, and if you decide to invest, your life takes you to a different level where you find your peace. Many are not aware, and many are aware but ignore it, and many are at peace with themselves. It is sometimes seen as an opportunity to connect with your inner self, to overcome regrets, or to repent, but most of all, it is a call from the creator showing the path to a higher being.

I started my own NGO called "Faith Save & Care Foundation" to help those in need and despair and get them back to a condition worth living. "Faith" is not a big organisation with lots of salaries to be paid and no work done, but a small one where all the donors were friends, colleagues, families, and everyone connected to them. My only work was fieldwork for the needy and communicating with the donors, and this kept the NGO running. My path was clear, as my main hurdle was my husband, and since my marriage was over and I was single again, nothing could stop me from doing what I wanted to do. I was always told that I was the one who needed help the most because I was mentally unstable. This I had to hear and live with for a long time, and I made a promise to myself that no one should go through the same and be told what I was told every single day. I also promised that I would keep Dad and Mom alive in me by following their path and their sayings because that was the only thing left with me given by them, and I wouldn't let anyone take anything away from me no matter what. Whenever I showed an interest in working for the needy or when I tried helping the distressed, I was shut down; all my resources were blocked, and I would be completely drained out, but I somehow managed to get away, and that's how I started my own NGO because the path was already chosen for me.

"The next evolutionary step for humankind is to move from man to kind."

I believe that all human beings have been created to serve each other; all of us do it in some form or another, sometimes unknowingly too. The wide disparity existing between people has always been a concern, so it is not by chance but destiny that's drawn me to work for the upliftment of the needy.

The sole aim is to support, and restructure the lives of women, focus on counselling, and strengthen distressed, depressed, and suicide victims. Restoring dignity to the downtrodden, helping families and children of the homeless, and enabling them to cope with the challenges of life, "Faith Save & Care Foundation" provided counselling sessions for distressed and suicide victims, enabling them to integrate back into society.

"We rise by lifting others." The others I mention here are people below the poverty line, people who haven't been able to meet the needs of their children and themselves; they live in the streets and under any shed that protects them from rain and cold; their children are born here and they grow up here; they eat when they find and earn by selling stuff in signals or by begging; but they are humans too, and if we provide them with food and a small amount of anyone's daily need, it only gives them a chance to live every day and brings hope to the children to look forward to a change.

It's a step taken to provide for the poor and roadside dwellers, which is only a step to make them find a different life for themselves. By providing them with the basic needs to survive and move ahead, the children who are pure and innocent don't have to beg; they have food and clothing—maybe just five percent of what we have—but at least it stops them from begging in the streets all day for a few coins.

Many steps have been taken to relocate the children and counsel the adults, to make them aware of living and working towards a better life, to get them off the streets, while trying to provide them with at least one basic meal a day. God provides; we are only his messengers.

I am a light worker; my role is to promote kindness, love, and optimism; help others on their healing paths; and serve the world as lights and pillars of hope. Light Workers: Contributing to the elevation of humankind's overall well-being.

You can grow by supporting and helping others. By doing this, you not only provide them with what they need to succeed, but you also start a positive reaction that may encourage and inspire others to follow your path. Helping others also enables you to grow in empathy and compassion, all of which may enhance your own personal growth journey. When you help others, you create a sense of peace and foster a supportive community. This sense of belonging can have a profound impact on your own well-being and overall happiness, as you become part of something greater than yourself. Additionally, by assisting others in their development, you may uncover hidden talents or strengths within yourself that you were previously unaware of, further improving your own personal growth.

A BROKEN MARRIAGE

When a woman moves on, it's not because she doesn't want to work it out. It's because she is exhausted from being in a one-sided relationship. Exhausted from being lied to, being taken advantage of, exhausted from being told that it's her fault every time, being put down in front of others. Exhausted from being grilled all the time she is useless. When a woman ends a marriage, it's because she has no choice left.

You are not born mentally tough. You choose to be. It's a skill that is learned and developed. The level of mental strength you will acquire will depend on the habits you build, how strong you are, and how much you believe in yourself. It's about embracing difficulty, discomfort, and what broke you.

Coping with a broken marriage can be very difficult and emotionally draining. A few things that kept me going: knowing that I had to survive for my children and be their strength. These things I will never forget because they gave me a new beginning and changed my whole outlook towards life. My life changed not because I went to court and got custody of my children but because I stayed focused and knew what I wanted, and no one could change that.

I had a very difficult marriage that lasted for eighteen long years. Every time I felt the need to put an end to it or mend it, it only got worse. I was with a man who was totally opposite of who I was. Though during the initial days of courtship, I felt it but kept it going, telling myself that opposites attract, which was the biggest lie.

I tried so hard to please him, to change my ways and pick up his ways, to step back and give him the lead, to have no self-respect or self-esteem, to totally ignore the values I'd learned, to only be good at domestic work, to cut off everyone who puts sense in me, to ensure my parents were never heard, to put down everything I was good at, to make the world believe that I was made by him and was nothing earlier, to demand money all the time, to make his family agree that it was okay for him to cheat on me, to allow him to regularly physically abuse me, to force me into doing things to prove my incompetence, to constantly tell me I was disliked by the whole world. And the last one that changed me was to make kids feel that he was doing the right thing. I was broken down mentally, physically, and emotionally to the point where I could not find myself back. I only wondered where I went wrong in life that I didn't remember what I was.

His affairs came into the open. Though I always ignored his flamboyant behaviour just for a little peace at home, people started talking about it and warning me. Even the kids witnessed a few instances, and to my surprise, they asked me to leave him. When I confronted him, it was the end of our marriage. In defence, he did everything he could to ruin my character. I put myself together and stood up. I resolved things one at a time, and the world slowly started looking better. But by this time, we were far apart, and the question of saving the marriage didn't arise.

By this time, there were other sorrows of losing my loved ones I was dealing with. So with everything coming on me at the same time, I was sure of what I wanted. I took a step up, dried my tears, and set out to conquer the world. I followed my heart and all that it taught me throughout my life. I didn't consider much what the repercussions would be; all I knew was that I needed to start all over again.

I'm putting down a few things that I remember helped me and are still with me. Although I have regained my strength, and my life has come back to normal, what got me to where I am today is what I will cherish for the rest of my life.

It is important to allow yourself some time to overcome the fact that your marriage did not work out. This may involve feeling sad, angry, happy, or confused. There is no right or wrong way to overcome the fact that your marriage is over, and it is important to allow yourself to feel your emotions, whatever kind they may be.

Also, talking to someone who is available and comforts you can be helpful in processing your emotions and coping with the challenges that come your way. You are not the first one to go through this, so there is the right advice and support available if you find help in the right people. Many people pretend to give the right advice but are not really what they pretend to be; they only mislead us and get us into deeper confusion. Such people not only need to be avoided but also whatever is said and heard needs to be removed from the system. We have a long way ahead of us and don't need such advice.

Before anyone judges you, they should step into your shoes and walk the life you are living, and if they get as far as you are, then maybe they will see how strong you really are.

Most importantly, take care of your physical and emotional health during this time. Make sure to get enough sleep, eat healthy foods, and exercise. What also helps to overcome stress is spending time in nature, listening to music, reading, or taking up a new hobby or interest.

Spending time with your children is the best. Get close to them by finding out what they missed out on during the difficult time of separation and listen to their opinions. They need healing too. Be their friend and assure them that life will only get better from here on. Children are sensitive; do not remind them of what has happened, but try to leave the past behind and move forward. Never share topics with kids that might hurt them, but make them part of the changes you make in life, take their advice, and appreciate it. Always praise them and make them feel important, knowing that they were also hurt in the divorce and need to be put together. To be rejected by someone they thought highly of is the biggest disappointment. Be their strength and saviour, even though you need it most. Give them what was taken away from you, like the confidence to always know their self-worth, the strength to chase their dreams, and the ability to know how deeply loved they are.

You might be tired, hungry, broken, overwhelmed, late, early, sad, dejected, and always alone, but you do it for them because you love them.

It takes time to heal from a broken marriage. Don't expect to feel better overnight. Be patient with yourself and allow yourself time to heal. It is easy to blame yourself for the breakdown of your marriage because this is what you were always told. Whatever might be the reason, but the one suffering is you, so it's you who needs a little more support at this time. It is easy to compare yourself to other couples who seem to be happy and successful. However, it is important to remember that everyone's journey is different. Just because your marriage didn't work out doesn't mean that you will always be the one to be blamed. Leave the past behind and move forward. Give yourself credit for how courageous you have been and how courageous you are now to choose the life you desire.

Love comes in different ways and in different forms; all you need is a heart to forgive and leave the past behind and move on. Life has given you a second chance, something very few people get. Consider yourself lucky, move on, and don't look back. Throughout all this, remember that you are not alone; regain your strength. Focus on your positive qualities and remind yourself that you are worthy of love and happiness. Never regret the love you gave someone, even if it didn't work out. Love always comes back in full circle; it will come in some shape or form.

Sometimes you have to lose everything to gain everything. Certain things have to end so better things can begin. Everything you have now is what you once wished for, and it's come to you because you stood strong. Never forget how broken you were, the hardships you have known, and the times you have lost yourself. But here you stand strong, still moving forward and growing stronger every day. The harsh lessons only made you stronger.

ABUSE

You just never know what someone is dealing with behind closed doors. No matter how happy someone looks, how loud their laughter is, or how big their smile is, there can still be a level of hurt that is indescribable. A person going through an abusive relationship never openly accepts it, thinking that it is normal. What is normal between two people is respect for one another without any kind of physical, verbal, sexual, emotional, or mental torture. If any of these are present in a relationship, the person causing it is an abuser, and the one receiving it is in an abusive relationship.

No matter what form it takes, abuse is never okay. It is a crime and a violation of human beings. It comes in many ways, and we never realise it until something feels not right, and we find ourselves in a shell.

Lucky are those who find help before they realise it. As for me, I was on my own, wishing that someone would show me the path. But it's always better if you find the path from within yourself. That way, you come out stronger and take the step for yourself because no one knows the harm caused better than you.

There were many ways by which I could understand that something was not right and that I might be in an abusive relationship. It took time for me to acknowledge and react, as I was made to believe that everything that felt wrong was actually normal things that happened in a family and needed no attention. It can also be repeated. At this time, what you feel from within is what's most important, and that's the inner voice you must listen to. You need to realise that normal things don't change you as an individual. If you have turned into a different person totally, which was never you, then something is not right. All these come to light once you see that you were born and raised differently by your parents, and now you are forced to become a different person altogether. It's your choice what you want to be and what you want to choose. If the values taught by your parents are strong and you can stand by them all alone, then half the battle is over.

I lost my identity. I told myself that I wasn't the person I was made to be. I didn't have to be a different person and accept the violence in my life. Instead, I started analysing the wrongs that kept happening to me from the start and started fighting back. This helped me gather courage and become more positive about myself, knowing that I was never wrong but was always made to feel wrong. A few things that changed the way I thought about myself still hold strong, and I will always be grateful to whoever made me do this because it changed my life forever.

Every time I was physically abused, I was told it would never happen again, promises after promises made but all in vain; it always happened again and with more vengeance. Everything seemed broken, and I had no answers to what was going on. All I was made to believe was that I deserved what was happening and that would be my life from then on. I had never seen this life before; every word uttered was a threat, an abuse, or making me feel worthless. Every action was projected towards teaching me a lesson. I was beaten up in front of the kids, hit for the smallest reasons, and made to starve. My helper, who was like my child, had to always beg him to spare me. But I refused to accept it; I told myself I deserved better, and I would not accept what was going on anymore. I will change my life and everything in it for my children and most of all for me. I stood strong to fight back and put in whatever it took physically, emotionally, and mentally. After a long struggle, I got out of that life. I never looked back and promised not to let my children go through what I had gone through. I promised to make them strong, not by putting someone else down, but by giving them my example.

Getting out of an abusive relationship is not easy, but it is possible. All you need is a little support every step of the way. Sometimes your strength becomes your biggest support when you know that it's your fight, and you have no one to lean on. The most important to start with is to get emotionally stronger; it is your answer to the hopes you have built over a shattered life.

Acknowledge your emotions. It's important to allow yourself to feel your emotions, even the difficult ones because that's how you move on. Practice self-compassion by being kind to yourself, just as you would want someone to treat you. Forgive yourself for your mistakes and learn from them. Set boundaries for yourself; don't be afraid to say no to things that you don't want to do. Most importantly, protect your time and energy, which will build you from now on.

Take care of yourself because you are the pillar to many now, and you can't break down. Taking care of your physical health will also benefit your emotional health. Spend time with positive people. Surround yourself with people who make you feel good about yourself. Avoid negative people who bring you down. It's time to let go of people you once thought were your friends but realised later that they weren't. Practice gratitude by taking some time each day to focus on the things you're grateful for. This can help you appreciate the good things in your life and feel more positive. As I mentioned earlier, if you're struggling to cope with your emotions, don't hesitate to seek help. Friends and family can help you develop emotional resilience, which is very important at this point in time.

Building emotional strength takes time and effort, but it's worth it. When you're emotionally strong, you're better able to handle the challenges of life and bounce back from setbacks.

Lastly, I owe myself a little apology for being in a space where I knew I was not respected, wanted, appreciated, loved, or valued. I am sorry for putting people who never appreciated me before myself. And instead of everything, I still stayed for the sake of the children. I know now that whatever pain I must have put my children through in the battle, today they are far from that world of seeing me get abused all the time. They will never accept this in their life.

Putting down few points to remember in an abusive relationship that you might not be aware of. It's good to learn early, you might suffer less.

Controlling Behaviour: everything about your life is controlled—your friends, family, finances, and even your daily activities. It's like your life is not yours, and you should be thankful for everything you have and owe it to him.

Jealousy: There is always a grudge held against you for all the things you had in the past and he didn't, and this creates a permanent anger in him against your lifestyle and is taken out on you in a negative way very often just to prove himself equal. He becomes overly jealous of your time and attention and accuses you of cheating and misbehaviour.

Intimidation: He uses threats or violence to scare you into doing what he wants. After a while, it becomes a way of life, and everything is based on that. He starts implementing it physically and makes you accept it as your fault.

Isolation: you are cut out from the rest of the world. He tries to keep you away from your friends and family, and he may make you feel like you can't trust anyone but him, and he is the only one. This way, you have no one to confront for support in times of need.

Humiliation: He puts you down or makes you feel bad about yourself, making you feel worthless and of no value. He breaks your confidence totally, to the point where it becomes difficult for you to get back to who you were. All your sources of strength are blocked, and you start living like a dependent with a barrier on all sides.

Blaming: He never takes responsibility for his actions, and he always blames you for the problems in the relationship. For everything that happens, there is only one answer, and that's how it would be.

Sex: Forcing penetration against your will and blaming you for being incompetent. You are also given warnings that this will be taken to court, which makes you feel guilty about his wrongdoing.

Physical: Many times, you are hit, beaten up, or manhandled. They are all the same and are done to control and dominate. It continues because he finds out your weaker side.

"Maybe the journey isn't so much about becoming anything. Maybe it's about unbecoming everything that really isn't you so that you can be who you were meant to be in the first place." - Paulo Coelho

AND

If you want to be happy for the rest of your life, learn to love yourself. Learn to prioritise yourself, learn to say no, learn to mind your business, learn not to care too much about unwanted things, and lastly, understand that you don't need everybody to like you.

Sometimes, it's better to just let things be. Let people go, don't fight for closure, don't ask for explanations, don't chase answers, and don't expect people to understand where you are coming from.

Give yourself credit. You're trying to grow while trying to heal. You are trying to forgive while trying to grieve. You are trying to search while trying to let go, and you are trying to love others while remembering how to love yourself. You are trying to do the best you can.

Just because it still hurts, doesn't mean you are not healing. Just because you have moments of overwhelming grief, doesn't mean your heart is not expanding. Healing hurts, and it's always worth it.

When I started a new life alone with my kids, there were many unanswered questions. I was also scared. I was a person who would not step into the kitchen once the lights were off, but circumstances changed me. I had a dog who would now follow me to the kitchen or anywhere in the house when the lights were off. This taught me that if no one, then God still follows you to look after you. Many times, when I tripped and fell, I got up on my own because I had to. Given a choice, I would have wanted to be picked up, and my wounds cleaned, as it was when I was a child. Now I have deeper wounds that only I can heal. Strong people break too. They just do it in silence, rebuild, and keep on moving forward.

Sometimes you have to lose everything to gain everything. Certain things have to end so better things begin. My life isn't over; it is just starting over. Few things will never be forgotten, like the silent battles I fought, the setbacks I had to overcome, the dark days when I had to wipe my own tears, but it all comes down to how much I loved my children and how every battle seemed small when it was fought for them.

Most people don't want to be part of the process; they just want to be part of the outcome. But the process is where you figure out who is worth being part of the outcome.

It is the one who stands by you when you've been let down, exhausted from overthinking, tired of being alone, and the strong one. Hope you receive all the love you share, and it comes to you as blessings, joy, stability, and support you deserve.

You don't have to be positive right away. Sit with your heavy feelings and understand them, know where they are coming from. Then, you can start understanding them better. Understand your emotions instead of ignoring them; it's this willpower that will help you improve. Be content that only a select few truly know and can see who you are. Let others speculate, create stories, and become lost in their own illusions, distortions, and fabrications. Stay present in your truth.

One night, after my prayers, I asked God why my friends hurt me and walked away after misusing our friendship. I was told that they were taking advantage of me because I was single. According to them, someone who is single and has gone through a lot in life can go to any extent to please others, so they don't go through the same pain again. If I retaliate, then I am in the wrong, and they will fight to break me down. I walked away to teach them a lesson and never looked back; I walked away because I finally learned my lesson. People don't abandon the people they love; they abandon the people they are using.

Move away from circumstances that drag you down. Get away from people who let you down. Life is always preparing you for something greater and more meaningful. So, if you are in a tough situation, don't get overwhelmed; you will learn something from it.

Most people aren't worth your time. But you are someone who loves from the heart, a believer, and someone who naturally cares. You try to touch other people's lives, to try to save them, no matter how they treat you. You care too much, love too much, feel too much, and that's why you get disappointed. One day it will all make sense, and you will understand that it was best to lose people who misinterpreted your feelings. You will be proud of yourself and thankful that you are not where you used to be in life. You have outgrown so much, and you are still learning. You have survived everything, and it has made you a better person. The more you love yourself, the more you will detach from things that don't love you.

Don't be afraid to get back up, to try again, to love again, to live again, and to dream again. Don't let a hard lesson harden your heart. Surround yourself with people who are committed to growth, who have values and integrity, who support you and want to see you rise. Surround yourself with those who have your back, not just on easy days, but also on the hard days. Surround yourself with people who care enough about you to tell you when you are slipping and who are strong enough to help you get back on track when you fall off.

Taking you back a few years when I had separated, everything seemed so heavy on my shoulders. Trying to balance out between starting everything anew and keeping the children motivated and happy, I brought home a little dog called Apple. He is a Shih Tzu and was two months old when I got him. I wanted to bring home a sense of happiness that was missing since we were all going through a rough patch. Apple was a cuddly, playful, loving puppy who later became everyone's little bundle of joy. He would eat with us, sleep with us, play with us, go out with us, laugh with us, cry with us, and later even started talking to us. I kept thinking about how someone could change our lives so much and how he seemed so human. He brought us joy and love, and everything started getting back to normal. I would sometimes ask him if he met mom in heaven and got trained to keep us happy. He would nod his head and say yes. Every time the kids were out, and I had to step out for work, I would notice that the floor near the entrance was always warm when I stepped in. It was Apple, who never moved from the door, waiting for us. Some things don't change; it might take time, but they always come back. Love found its way back, and it was a kinder, better kind of love.

I told my friend Dhananjay that there is one song that reminds me of mom and dad, and even when everything seems down, this song makes me smile. He wrote it down for me, and I'm sharing a line with you too:

"Ae dil hai mushkil jeena yahan,

Zara hat ke, zara bach ke, yeh hai Bombay meri jaan."

GRATITUDE

I'd like to thank everyone who has ever said an encouraging word to me or taught me what I consider a life lesson. I heard all that you said and it was meaningful to me. I love you Babe and Hasan, my siblings and my dear departed parents and sister, who I miss every day.

Thank you to everyone in my Running Buddies group who keep me going, and my heartfelt thanks to those who support my NGO, Faith Save & Care Foundation for the empowerment to help others. Lastly, I want to thank my friend Amit for encouraging me to write this book, and my good friend Megha for always being there for me.

Lastly, my two daughters for being my lifeline.

Thank you Dynaesh for the cover design.

www.ingramcontent.com/pod-product-compliance
Lightning Source LLC
LaVergne TN
LVHW091052150826
845673LV00002B/549

* 9 7 9 8 8 9 1 8 6 3 4 6 0 *